Spiralizer

COOKBOOK & GUIDE

Learn to Create Tasty Meals Using Your Spiralizer!!

vigor&belle

© 2016

Follow us on Social Media!

Connect with other people, get the latest info, discuss the most recent vigor&belle products or simply show your love for the vigor&belle brand!

Facebook
Connect and become friends with other fans, or comment, discuss the latest posts and releases from vigor&belle.

Instagram
Follow vigor&belle on Instagram for even more healthy recipes, lifestyle and beauty ideas.

Pinterest
Pin, like and comment your favorite vigor&belle recipes and beauty trends.

TABLE OF CONTENTS

Introduction:

If you're the proud owner of a shiny new Spiralizer, you're no doubt keen to start using it. But before you do, you should be aware that this little kitchen gadget can offer you much more than you think.

While some people may limit themselves to making carrot noodles and cucumber ribbons, there are those who use the Spiralizer to its full potential. This recipe book will help you to do just that, and ensure that you can enjoy 100 different meals that can add a bit of excitement to meal times.

Whether you're trying to encourage your children to eat more vegetables, or you simply want to try something new, let this recipe book show you how it's done. Here you will find a whole host of recipes that will enable you to use your new Spiralizer during the meal creation process. Take a look at the recipes contained within this book, and learn how to use your Spiralizer to its full potential.

Make meal times more exciting, enjoy eating delicious meals that have been prepared in ways you could never have imagined!

Breakfast Ideas

Egg, Bacon And Mushroom Potato Noodles
Serves: 1

Ingredients:
1 sweet potato (Peeled)
Cooking spray
2 strips bacon
1 tbsp parsley (Chopped)
1 tbsp olive oil
1 Tbsp Parmesan (Shredded)
½ red bell pepper (Chopped)
1 garlic clove (Minced)
½ red onion (Chopped)
1 egg
6 button mushrooms (Quartered)
Sprinkle chili powder
Sprinkle garlic powder
Sprinkle oregano
Salt & Pepper

Method
Spiralize the sweet potato into noodles, and set to one side. In a large skillet, add the bacon, and cook until it's reached your preferred texture. Set to one side. Add half the olive oil to your skillet, and then add the garlic powder and noodles. Season, and cook for about 5 minutes, or until the noodles are soft. Once the

noodles are done, place them on a plate and set to one side.

Take a skillet, and add the remainder of the olive oil, add the garlic, and stir for 30 seconds. Now add the peppers, onions, chili, and a little pepper. Stir well, and cook for 2-3 minutes, or until the onions are soft. Now add the mushrooms and cook for 3 more minutes. Add the bacon, stir well, and then spoon the mushroom mix on top of the noodles. Allow the mushroom mix to sit for a few minutes. Take your egg, and fry it until it's cooked to your satisfaction. Once the egg is done, place it on top of the mushrooms. Season with the Parmesan and parsley. Serve.

Goats Cheese Buns With Eggs
Serves: 3

Ingredients:
1 Yukon potato (Peeled)
1 tbsp olive oil
Cooking spray
6 cucumber slices
1 tsp garlic powder
1 tbsp dill (Chopped)
Salt & pepper
4 ounces goat cheese
4 eggs

Method
Spiralize your potato and turn it into noodles. Now add the noodles to a skillet that's been sprayed with cooking spray. Turn the heat to a medium setting, and season. Sprinkle the garlic powder over the noodles, and allow to cook for about 5 minutes, or until the noodles are a little brown.

Remove the noodles from the skillet, and place them in a bowl. Add 1 egg to the bowl, and combine with the noodles. Add the noodle mix to three small bowls, and fill them up halfway with noodles. Now take some wax paper, and place it over the bowls, and then place a can over each of the bowls to push the noodles down. Place in the refrigerator for about 10 minutes. Take the noodles are squashed, hold the bowls over the skillet and turn them over and allow the noodles to fall out. Cook the noodles for a few minutes on each side. Once the are done, set to one side.

Now add the dill and goats cheese to a blender, and pulse until they are nicely combined. Now add the eggs to a skillet and fry them. While the eggs are cooking, add the cucumber and goats cheese to the noodle buns. Once the eggs are done, divide them between the noodle buns, placing them directly on top. Season and serve.

Oatmeal With Apples And Cranberries

Serves: 2-3

Ingredients:
3 packs instant oats (Water added)
1 ounce goats cheese (Crumbled)
1 apple
4 tbsp cranberries (Dried)
¼ cup almond milk (Unsweetened)
3 tbsp walnuts (Chopped)

Method
Add the oats to 2-3 bowls, and Spiralize the apple into a fine noodle. Add the apple to the oats and stir well. Now top with the cheese, cranberries and walnuts. Pour the almond milk over the top, serve.

Parsnip Waffles

Serves: 2

Ingredients:
½ tbsp olive oil
3 tbsp chive
2 parsnips (Peeled)
1 egg (Beaten)
¼ tsp garlic powder
Salt & pepper

Method
Preheat your waffle iron. Spiralize the parsnips into thick noodles, and add the oil to a skillet. As soon as the oil starts to heat up, add the noodles, garlic powder and salt and pepper. Cook for about 5 minutes, or until the noodles are thoroughly cooked.

Once the noodles are done, add them to a bowl. Now stir in the chives and eggs, and toss well. Spray the waffle iron with the cooking spray, and add the parsnip mix. Push the mix down well so it sits nicely in the waffle iron. Cook as per the manufacturer's instructions. Serve.

Cabbage Burrito With Noodles

Serves: 2

Ingredients:
2 savoy cabbage leaves
4 eggs (Beaten)
1 avocado (Cubed)
1 sweet potato
Salt & pepper
4 bacon slices

Method
Spiralize your sweet potato and make it into thick noodles. Add the avocado to a bowl, and mash well. Season with the salt & pepper, and then spread the avocado mix over the cabbage leaves.

Take a skillet and cook the bacon on a medium heat. Cook as per your preferences, and then set to one side. Now drain off half of the bacon fat, and then add the noodles to the skillet. Cook for about 5 minutes, or until the noodles have started to wilt.

When the noodles are done, spoon them on top of the avocado, and set to one side. Add the eggs to the skillet, and stir so they become scrambled. Once the eggs are done, spoon them onto the noodles. Take the bacon, and place it on top of the eggs. Roll the cabbage leaves around the eggs to form a burrito. Serve.

Breakfast Frittata With Sweet Potato & Kale

Serves: 6

Ingredients:
1 tbsp olive oil
5 ounces baby arugula
2 cups kale (Chopped)
½ cup goats cheese (Crumbled)
¼ tsp red pepper flakes
8 eggs (Beaten)
Salt & pepper
1 sweet potato

Method
Preheat your oven to 425 Fahrenheit. Spiralize the sweet potato so it creates thick noodles. Heat half the olive oil in a skillet and add the pepper flakes, salt & pepper and kale. Cook on a medium-high heat for about 3 minutes or until the kale has wilted. Once the kale is done, set it to one side. Now add the rest of the olive oil to the skillet, and and place the noodles in there. Season, and toss, allowing the noodles to cook. Cook for about 7 minutes, or until the noodles are almost completely wilted. Add the kale, stir, and then pour the eggs over the top. Season and cook for 2 more minutes, or until the eggs are set at the bottom. Now add the goats cheese, and allow them to be covered in the eggs.

Add the frittata to the oven, and cook for about 10 minutes, or until the eggs are done. Remove from the oven, and serve.

Breakfast Butternut Squash Risotto With Bacon & Eggs

Serves: 4

Ingredients:
4 bacon slices
¼ cup Havarti cheese (Shredded)
4 eggs
½ cup mild cheese (Shredded)
2 tbsp parsley (Minced)
½ cup chicken broth
1 butternut squash (Peeled)
Salt & pepper
1 tbsp olive oil
2 garlic cloves (Minced)

Method
Spiralize the butternut squash to thick noodles are formed, then add them to a food processor, and pulse until they look a little like rice. Set to one side. Now take a skillet, and add the bacon, cook on a medium-high heat until the bacon is crispy, and set to one side.

Add 1 tbsp olive oil to a pot, and once it's starting to heat up, add the garlic, and cook for about 30-40 seconds, or until you're able to smell it. Now add the butternut squash and season. Stir and allow to cook for about 2 minutes. Add the chicken broth, and turn the heat to low and simmer. Cook for about 10 minutes, or until a lot of the broth has reduced. Remove from the heat, and then add the cheese, stir well until all of the cheese is melted. Add the bacon, stir again, and then add the eggs to the skillet. Cook until the eggs are done. Add the risotto to a bowl, top with the eggs, sprinkle the parsley on top, and serve.

Dragon Fruit Breakfast Pudding
Serves: 1

Ingredients:
1 dragon fruit (Peeled, skin saved)
2 tsp lemon juice
1 tbsp chia seeds
5 tbsp water

Method
Add the lemon juice, water and chia seeds to a bow, and allow to soak for about 10 minutes. Spiralize the dragon fruit so you have spaghetti-like noodles. Place the dragon fruit back into the skin. Top with the chia seeds, and serve.

Sweet Potato Breakfast Burrito
Serves: 2

Ingredients:
1 sweet potato
2 tsp cilantro
1 tbsp olive oil
1 avocado (Diced)
Salt & pepper
½ cup salsa
2 eggs
8 egg whites

Method
Spiralize the potatoes so you create small noodles.
Take 2 tsp of olive oil, and add it to a pan. Turn the
heat up to medium, and add the noodles. Cook the
noodles for about 5 minutes, or until they start to
soften. Add the salt and pepper to the noodles.

Now fill a pot with water, and heat on a medium-high
heat. Once the water starts to simmer, crack the 2
eggs, and cover the pot. Turn the heat off, and give the
eggs the chance to cook for about 4 minutes, or until
the center of the eggs are soft.

Take the remaining olive oil and heat it in a pan on a
medium-high heat. Scramble the egg whites, and then
set to one side. Add the noodles to a bowl and spoon
the salsa in. Mix well, and then add the scrambled

eggs, and mix again. Add the noodles to a few bowls, top with the avocado and cilantro, and serve.

Chickpea & Potato Noodle Breakfast Tacos

Serves: 4

Ingredients:
1 avocado (Insides scooped out)
3 tbsp scallions (Sliced)
1 ½ tbsp cilantro
4 corn tortillas
1 lime (Juiced)
¼ cup BBQ sauce
1 tsp Jalapeño (Minced)
½ cup chickpeas
Salt & pepper
3 eggs (Beaten)
2 tsp olive oil
Cooking spray
1 sweet potato (Peeled)
¼ tsp paprika

Method
Add the avocado, cilantro, lime juice, Jalapeño, and salt & pepper to a food processor. Pulse the ingredients until they are creamy. Now heat a skillet on a medium-high heat, and add the noodles. Now sprinkle in the paprika and salt & pepper. Cook for about 5 minutes, and toss now and again.

Take another skillet turn it up to a medium high heat and add the cooking spray. Scramble the eggs, and then add the BBQ sauce and chickpeas. Stir until the chickpeas are warm. Now take 2 of your tortillas and place them on a plate next to each other. Take half the avocado mix, and spread it on the tortillas. Add the noodles, and the chickpeas and eggs. Garnish with the scallions, and then repeat with the remaining tortillas. Serve.

Spiralized Scallion Cake
Serves: 2

Ingredients:
2 bacon slices (Chopped)
2 tsp olive oil
2 scallions (Chopped)
1 egg (Beaten)
½ pound red potato
Salt & pepper

Method
Spiralize the potato and make thin noodles, set to one side. Add the bacon and all but 1 tsp of scallions to a skillet that's on a medium heat, and cook for about 5 minutes, or until the bacon is starting to turn a little brown. Add the bacon to the noodles, and mix well. Season with the salt and pepper, and allow to cool for a few minutes. Once a few minutes are up, add the egg, and stir once more.

Now take a skillet, and heat the noodle mix on a medium-low heat. Pat the mixture down using a spatula, or a spoon. Cook the noodle mix for about 5 minutes, and then turn the mixture over, and cook on the other side. Once the potato cake is done, place it on a plate, and sprinkle the remaining scallions over the top. Serve.

Chocolate Chip Potato Noodles
Serves: 2

Ingredients:
1 sweet potato (Peeled)
Cooking spray
½ tsp cinnamon
2 tbsp dark chocolate
1 egg (Beaten)
½ cup blueberries

Method
Place the sweet potato in your Spiralizer and make thick noodles

Heat your waffle iron, and then heat some olive oil in a skillet. As soon as the oil is starting to heat up, add the sweet potatoes, and sprinkle the cinnamon and a bit of salt on top. Toss, and cook for about 10 minutes, or until the noodles are thoroughly cooked.

Once the noodles are done, add them to a bowl, and stir in the chocolate and egg. Spray the waffle iron with cooking spray, and then add the noodles, ensuring they are tightly packed in. Cook using the waffle manufacturer's instructions. Once the waffles are done, place them on a plate, and serve.

Scrambled Tofu With Broccoli Noodles
Serves: 3

Ingredients:
2 broccoli stems
Salt & pepper
14 ounces tofu (Extra firm, crumbled)
1 tsp turmeric
2 tbsp olive oil
1 tsp cumin
½ onion (Diced)
1 red bell pepper (Diced)
2 cloves garlic (Minced)

Method
Spiralize the broccoli so it makes spaghetti-like noodles. Heat a pot of water and allow it to boil. Add the noodles and cook for about 2 minutes, or until they're al dente. Now take a skillet, and heat the oil on a medium heat. Then add the peppers, onion and garlic, and cook for about 3 minutes, or until the vegetable have turned soft. Add the cumin and stir well. Then add the turmeric, noodles and tofu, and stir again. Season, and then cook for a few more minutes so the tofu is heated. Serve.

Sweet Potato Pumpkin Spice Waffles
Serves: 1

Ingredients:
1 sweet potato
1 tbsp maple syrup
1 tsp pumpkin spice
1 egg (Beaten)
Cooking spray

Method
Spiralize the sweet potato to create spaghetti noodles.
Heat your waffle iron and then take a large skillet.
Add the cooking spray to the skillet and turn the heat
to medium. Add the sweet potatoes and cook for 10
minutes. Once the noodles are soft, add them to a
bowl and stir in the pumpkin spice. Now add the egg
and stir in thoroughly. Spray your waffle iron with
cooking spray, and add the noodles, packing them in
tightly. Cook as per the manufacturer's instructions.
Once the waffles are done, remove them from the
waffle iron, place on a plate, and pour the maple syrup
over the top. Serve.

Pizza Muffins With Potato Noodles

Makes: 12

Ingredients:
1 tbsp olive oil
2 tbsp Parmesan (Shredded)
2 Yukon potatoes (Peeled)
12 slices turkey pepperoni
Salt & pepper
1 cup mozzarella (Shredded)
½ tsp garlic powder
½ cup turkey pepperoni (Sliced)
12 eggs
¼ tsp onion powder
1 cup diced tomatoes (Drained)
½ tsp cilantro
½ tsp oregano

Method

Preheat your oven to 375 Fahrenheit. Spiralize the potatoes to create thick noodles. Add the oil to a skillet and heat on a medium heat. Add the noodles, garlic, and salt and pepper, toss well. Cook for 5 minutes, or until the boodles are al dente. Toss occasionally.

Take a muffin tray, and coat with cooking spray. Divide the noodles between the tray, and pack them in thoroughly until each section is half full.

Beat the eggs in a bowl, then add the onion powder, tomatoes, basil and oregano. Stir well. Now add the salt and pepper, along with the diced pepperoni, and stir again. Pour the mixture into the muffin tray, until each of the sections are two-thirds full. Sprinkle the mozzarella on top, add a slice of pepperoni, and place the muffins in the oven. Cook for about 20 minutes, or until the eggs are set. Once the muffins are done, sprinkle the Parmesan on top, and serve.

Eggs With Sweet Potato Noodles & Hollandaise

Serves: 3

Ingredients:
1 sweet potato
3 tbsp coconut oil (Melted)
Olive oil spray
1 chipolte pepper
½ tsp sea salt
1 tsp adobo sauce
¼ tsp garlic powder
Salt & pepper
1 tbsp lemon juice
1 avocado (Cubed)
2 egg yolks
3 eggs
1 tbsp cilantro (Chopped)

Method
Spiralize the potato to create thick noodles, and set to one side. Preheat your oven to 425 Fahrenheit, and add the noodles to a baking sheet. Sprinkle the salt, pepper, and garlic powder on the top, and then the avocado cubes. Roast in the oven for 10 minutes, or until the noodles are done.

Add the yolks, sea salt, chipotle pepper, lemon juice and adobo sauce to a blender, blend for 8-10 seconds, or until smooth, now blend on a medium setting, and then add the coconut oil. Blend a little more, and once

Apple Noodle Cinnamon Pancakes
Serves: 3

Ingredients:
4 eggs (Beaten)
Maple syrup
2 bananas
¼ tsp cinnamon
2 tsp coconut oil
1 apple

Method
Spiralize the apple to create thick noodles, and set to
one side. Now add the bananas to a bowl and mash.
Add the eggs, and stir well. Heat a skillet on a
medium-high heat, spray with cooking spray, and add
the egg mix to it, 2 tbsp at a time. Cook the pancakes
for 1 minute or until it's set at the bottom. Flip over,
and cook on the other side, and place on a plate.
Repeat using the rest of the mixture. Add the coconut
oil to the skillet, and add the apples and cinnamon.
Cook for 2 minutes, or until the apples are wilted.
Divide the pancakes between 3 plates, and add the
apple on top. Pour over some maple syrup, and serve.

it's thickened, set it to one side. Take a sauce pot, and fill it halfway with water, and then bring it to a simmer. Stir the water and create a whirlpool, crack the eggs and add them to the whirlpool. Allow to cook for 3 minutes, and then set to one side.

Place the noodles on a plate, and top with the eggs, and drizzle the sauce on top. Serve with the cilantro sprinkled on top.

Breakfast Pie With Potato Noodles, Eggs & Avocado

Serves: 2

Ingredients:
2 Yukon gold potatoes
Parsley
Salt & pepper
Sriracha
1 tsp garlic powder
½ avocado (Sliced)
2 eggs

Method
Spiralize the potatoes to create ribbons, and set to one side. Preheat the oven to 400 Fahrenheit, and add the noodles, garlic, pepper, salt and olive oil to a bow. Toss well. Spray a pie pan with cooking spray, and add the noodles. Bake until they are golden brown, or for 45 minutes. Remove the noodles from the pie pan when they are done, and place on a plate. Add the eggs to a skillet, and cook until they are set. Add the eggs on top of the noodles, and sprinkle avocado, sriracha, and parsley on top. Serve.

Snacks & Side Dishes

Sweet Potato Fries
Serves: 1

Ingredients:
1 tsp cumin
1 sweet potato
1 tsp smoked paprika
1 tsp black pepper
1 tsp onion powder
1 tsp garlic powder

Method
Preheat your oven to 415 Fahrenheit. Spiralize your sweet potato and create thin strings. Place the strings in a bowl, and add the rest of the ingredients. Mix well, and add the strings to the bowl. Toss to coat the strings in the spice mix. Now line a baking sheet, and spread the potato strings out. Place in the oven, and cook for about 20 minutes, or until the potato strings are a little brown at the edges. Serve.

Chipotle Lime Curly Fries
Serves: 4

Ingredients:
2 sweet potatoes
Chipolte Aioli
Cooking spray
Salt & pepper

Method
Preheat your oven to 400 Fahrenheit. Spiralize the potatoes as thinly as you can. Add the potatoes to a baking sheet that's been lined, and spread them out evenly. Spray with the cooking spray, and season. Bake in the oven for about 30 minutes, or until the fries are crispy. Remove the fries from the oven when they're done, and top with some chipolte aioli. Serve.

Baked Potato Chips
Serves: 6-8

Ingredients:
4 potatoes
1 tbsp oil
3 tbs salt

Method
Spiralize the potatoes so they are cut into ribbons. Grease a baking sheet, and add the potatoes to the sheet. You may need to lean the potato strips on their side, in order to fit them all on.

Sprinkle the salt over the potato chips, and bake in the oven for about 20 minutes, or until they are a nice golden brown. Serve.

Cinnamon Apple Chips
Serves: 3-4

Ingredients:
2 apples
¼ tsp salt
1 tbsp cinnamon
Cooking spray

Method
Spiralize your apples so thin noodles are created. Now preheat the oven to 250 Fahrenheit, and onto a baking sheet, add the apples, salt, cinnamon and cooking spray. Toss well to combine. Cook for 2 hours, or until the apples are crisp. You should toss the apples a few times during the cooking process.

Once the chops are done allow them to cool, and serve.

Carrot Ribbons With Rosemary Sauce
Serves: 6-8

Ingredients:
4 carrots (Peeled)
¼ tsp salt
1 tbsp butter
½ tsp parsley
½ tsp rosemary

Method
Spiralize the carrot to create ribbons. Now fill a pan
with an inch of water, and bring to the boil. Place the
ribbons in a steamer basket, and add to the pan.
Cover, and allow the ribbons to steam for 3 minutes,
or until they are a little crisp. Add the parsley, salt,
butter, and rosemary to a bowl, and stir well. Once the
carrot ribbons are done, add them to the bowl and
lightly toss them so ensure they are coated. Serve.

Onion Bhajis
Makes: 12-14

Ingredients:
2 onions
Coconut oil
¾ cup chickpea flour
5 tbsp water
½ tsp baking powder
1 tsp lemon juice
1 tsp salt
2 tbsp cilantro
1 tsp cumin
1 green chili (Deseeded, chopped)
½ tsp turmeric

Method
Spiralize the onions to make flat noodles, and set to one side. Add the turmeric flour, lemon juice, baking powder, chili, salt, and cumin to a bowl. Whisk well, and add the water. Stir to create a thick batter.

As soon as the batter has turned thick, add the onion, and stir well. Using your hands, make 12-14 balls, and flatten them a little to create a bhaji shape.

Heat a skillet with a half inch of coconut in it on a medium heat. Once the oil is hot, add the batter, and cook for about 1 minute on each side. The bhajis are done when they're golden brown. Repeat with the rest of the batter, and serve.

Cucumber & Sesame Salad

Serves: 2

Ingredients:
1 Cucumber (Seedless)
1 tbsp cilantro
1 carrot
½ scallion (Sliced)
½ tsp salt
½ tbsp toasted sesame seeds
1 tbsp rice vinegar
Sprinkle red pepper flakes
½ tsp lime juice
½ tsp sesame oil
1 ½ tbps honey

Method
Spiralize the carrot and cucumber to create long noodles. Add the cucumber to a strainer along with the salt. Toss well, and let the cucumber drain for about 10 minutes. Now take a bowl, and add the lime juice, red pepper flakes, sesame oil, sesame seeds, and vinegar. Stir well to combine.

Add the carrot and cucumber noodles to a bowl, and then spoon in about 1 tbsp of the sesame dressing. Stir well, and then add the cilantro and scallions, and a few more sesame seeds. Serve.

Beet Noodles With Cheese Dip
Serves: 4

Ingredients:
2 beets
¼ tsp pepper
2 tbsp oil
2 tsp oil
1 ¼ tsp salt
4 ounces cheese (Preferably goats cheese)
Sprinkle pepper
½ cup mayonnaise
1 tsp thyme
2 tsp balsamic vinegar
2 tsp honey

Method
Preheat your oven to 400 Fahrenheit. Spiralize your beets to create thin noodles. Now take the noodles, and place them in a bowl. Add 1 tsp salt, pepper, and 2 tbsp oil. Toss to combine.

Take 3 baking sheets, and add 1 tsp of oil to each of them. Rub the oil into the sheets, and then place them in the oven. Heat the oil for about 3 minutes, and then remove the baking sheets from the oven. Add half of the noodles to each of the sheets, and place them in the oven for about 30 minutes, or until the beets start to go a little brown. Allow the noodles to cool for a few minutes.

Now take the cheese, mayonnaise, vinegar, honey, thyme, ¼ tsp salt, and pepper, and add them to a blender or food processor. Blend gently to combine. Set to one side. Add the beet noodles to a plate, and pour the cheese dip in a shallow dish. Place the dish to the side of the beets, and serve.

Sweet Potato Rosemary Chips
Serves: 4

Ingredients:
3 tbsp butter (Melted)
Salt & pepper
3 tbsp olive oil
1 shallot (Peeled, sliced)
3 sweet potatoes
¼ tsp rosemary

Method
Spiralize the potatoes to create thin slices, and set to one side. Add the rosemary, oil and butter to a bowl, and stir well. Now pour 2 tbsp this mix into a baking dish. Add the slices of potato so they're stood on their edges. Take the shallot, and add a slice here and there, making sure they're lodged between the potatoes.

Take the rest of the butter mix, and spread it over the top of the potato slices. Season, and cover with foil. Add to the oven, and cook for 1 hour at 400 Fahrenheit. Remove the foil, and cook for about 10 more minutes, or until the potato tops are starting to turn a little brown. Serve.

Cucumber Salad With Sesame & Miso

Serves: 4

Ingredients:
2 English cucumbers
1 tbsp black sesame seeds (Toasted)
1 ½ cups edamame (Shelled)
2 carrots (Julienne)
2 ½ tbsp white miso
½ tsp soy sauce
1 ½ tbsp warm water
2 tsp lemon juice
2 tbsp rice vinegar
1 tbsp sesame oil
1 tsp sesame oil
1 tbsp ginger (Grated)
1 tsp ginger (Grated)
1 tbsp maple syrup

Method
Spiralize the cucumber to make ribbons, and add to a bowl. Add the carrots and edamame to the same bowl, and toss to combine. Now take another bowl, and add the miso and water, stir until the mix is smooth. Add the remaining ingredients, and whisk well.

Add the dressing to the vegetables, and toss again. Serve.

Sweet Potato Latkes

Serves: 2

Ingredients:
5 sweet potatoes (Peeled)
2 tbsp olive oil
½ cup scallions (Chopped)
1 egg (Beaten)
Salt & pepper
2 cloves garlic (Crushed)

Method
Spiralize the sweet potato to create thin noodles. Now add the potatoes, eggs, salt & pepper, garlic and scallions to a bow, and mix well.

Add 1 tsp of the olive oil to a skillet, and heat it on a low heat. Now add some sweet potato to the skillet, and press it down gently to flatten. Cook until the latkes are slightly brown on each side (This should take about 3 minutes per side). Repeat with the remaining noodles. Serve.

Vegetable Fritters
Makes: 12

Ingredients:
2 cups zucchini
½ cup scallions (Sliced)
2/3 cup all-purpose flour
2 garlic cloves (Minced)
2 cups carrots
2 eggs (Beaten)
vegetable oil
Salt
1/8 tsp pepper

Method
Spiralize the zucchini and carrots to create thin noodles. Then add the zucchini to a colander, and sprinkle it with some salt. Allow the zucchini to sit for about 10 minutes. Once 10 minutes is up, and the zucchini to a towel, and squeeze it well to let the water out. Now add it to a bowl, along with the rest of the ingredients apart from the vegetable oil. Add 1/8 tsp salt, and stir well.

Place some paper towels on a plate, and then heat a pan on a medium-high heat. Add some vegetable oil, and as soon as it starts to heat up, take 3 tbsp of the fritter mix, and add it to the pan. Flatten the mix down, and add more to the pan. Cook for about 3 minutes on one side, then about 2 minutes on the other. Cook until they're crispy and brown. Once cooked, add them to the paper towel, season, and repeat with the rest of the mix. Serve.

Spiraled Sweet Potatoes With Cinnamon
Serves: 3

Ingredients:
3 skewers
3 tbsp olive oil
3 sweet potatoes
3 tbsp sugar
1 tsp cinnamon
3 tbsp sugar
1 tbsp corn starch

Method
Preheat your oven to 400 Fahrenheit, and spray a baking sheet with some cooking spray. Spiralize the potatoes to create thin slices, and then stick them onto the skewers. Now add the skewered potatoes to a zip lock bag, and pour in the corn starch. Close the bag, and shake it well so the corn starch coats the potatoes.

Now remove the skewers from the bag, and place them on the baking sheet. Drizzle with the olive oil, and sprinkle the sugar and cinnamon on top. Add to the oven, and cook for about 15 minutes on both sides. Once 15 minutes is up, turn the broiler on, and cook them for another 2 minutes. Cool, and serve.

Onion Strings With Horseradish Sauce

Serves: 4

Ingredients:
Vegetable oil
1 tsp black pepper
1 tsp salt
1 vidalia onion
1 ½ cup cornmeal
1 ¼ cup buttermilk
½ cup mayonnaise
Sprinkle black pepper
2 tbsp horseradish sauce
Sprinkle salt
Juice ½ lemon

Method
Spiralize the onion to make thin noodles, and set to one side. Now take the buttermilk, and add it to a bowl. Add the onions, and mix well.

Take a pie plate, and add the salt, pepper, and cornmeal, and toss to combine, Now heat the vegetable oil in a pot, and once it's reached about 350 Fahrenheit, take a handful of the onion rings, but not the buttermilk, and coat them in cornmeal. Then, shale off the excess buttermilk, and add them to the pot. Fry each lot of onion strings for about 1 minute 30 seconds until they are crispy and slightly golden. Drain the oil off the strings, and set to one side. Repeat with the rest of the onion strings.

Now take the mayonnaise, horseradish, lemon juice, and some salt & pepper, and add them to a bowl, mix well, and serve with the onion strings.

Parsnip & Paprika Chips
Serves: 4

Ingredients:
2 pounds parsnips (Peeled)
Smoked paprika
4 cups vegetable coil
Salt

Method
Spiralize the parsnips so they make thin noodles, and place them in a bowl. Using your hands, toss the parsnips so they become unstuck. Now heat the oil in a pot, to 365 Fahrenheit. Once the oil has reached the desired temperature, add some of the parsnips, but not too many at a time. Cook for 35-45 seconds, and then place the parsnips on paper towels so they can drain. Sprinkle with a bit of salt, and repeat with the rest of the parsnips. Once all the parsnips are done, sprinkle the paprika on top, and serve.

Soups, Stews & Salads

Spinach & Chickpea Noodle Stew
Serves: 2

Ingredients:
1 tbsp olive oil
1 cup rice (Cooked)
1 clove garlic (Chopped)
¼ cup almond flakes (Toasted)
½ red onion (Chopped)
1 cup spinach
1 ½ tsp cumin
¾ cup chickpeas (Cooked)
¾ tsp smoked paprika
½ tbsp tomato paste
Sprinkle cayenne pepper
1 can chopped tomatoes
¼ tsp salt
½ zucchini
½ red bell pepper
1 ½ tsp brown sugar
Sprinkle black pepper

Method
Spiralize the red bell pepper to create thin pieces, then switch blades, and spiralize the zucchini to create thin noodles. Heat the oil in a skillet, and add the onion. Fry for a few minutes on a low heat, or until the onion is translucent. Now add the garlic, and stir well, until

it's soft. Add the rest of the spices, and sugar and stir again. Add the red pepper and zucchini, and fry the ingredients of the pan for a few more minutes.

As soon as the sauce starts to get a little thick, season with the black pepper. Now add the chickpeas, spinach. Stir well, and place the lid on the pan so the spinach can steam. After a few minutes, remove the lid, stir well, and serve.

Sriracha & Lime Chicken Soup
Serves: 2

Ingredients:
1 chicken breast (Sliced)
2 lime wedges
4 cups chicken broth
1 tsp sriracha
1 tsp cilantro
¼ tsp garlic powder
½ tbsp lime juice
1/8 tsp cumin
1 zucchini

Method
Spiralize your zucchini to create thick or thin noodles, depending on your preference. Add your chicken to a pot, and place on a medium-high heat. Now add the garlic, cumin and broth, and bring to the boil. Once the pot is boiling, reduce the heat and allow to simmer. Keep simmering until the chicken is fully cooked (This should take about 10 minutes.)

When the chicken is done, add the lime juice and noodles. Stir well, and simmer for another 3 minutes. Spoon the soup into bowls, sprinkle with the cilantro and add some sriracha sauce. Serve.

Chicken & Zucchini Noodle Curry

Serves: 4

Ingredients:
2 tsp turmeric
Juice ½ lemon
1 tsp coriander
4 zucchinis
1 tsp cumin
1 red pepper (Diced)
1 tsp salt
3 carrots (Chopped)
2 cloves garlic (Minced)
1 ¼ cups coconut milk
1 inch ginger (Shredded)
1 cup bone broth
2 tbsp coconut oil
1 ½ pounds chicken (Chopped)

Method
Spiralize the noodles to create noodles with the thickness of your choice. Now take a bowl, and add the coriander, salt, turmeric, garlic, cumin, and ginger, and mix well. Set to one side. Melt the coconut oil in a skillet on a medium-high heat, and then sauté the chicken for about 5 minutes, or until the pinkness has gone from the inside. Once the chicken is done, add the spices and stir well. Cook for one more minute. Add the coconut milk and bone broth, and stir again.

Now add the pepper and carrots, and bring the ingredients to a boil. Once it's reached boiling point, reduce the heat to a simmer. Simmer for 5 minutes, and add the zucchini. Cook for 5 more minutes, or until the chicken is thoroughly cooked. Add the lemon juice, and serve.

Zucchini & Chicken Soup
Serves: 2-3

Ingredients:
2 tbsp olive oil
2 cups cooked chicken (Shredded)
½ white onion (Chopped)
4 thyme sprigs
½ tsp oregano
2 celery stalks (Chopped lengthwise, halved)
1 carrot (Peeled)
1 zucchini
1 ½ garlic cloves (Minced)
1 tsp parsley
4 cups chicken broth

Method
Spiralize the zucchini to make flat noodles, and the carrot to make thin noodles. Heat the oil in a pot on a medium heat. Once the oil has started to heat up, add the celery, onion and garlic. Season, and stir. Cook for about 5 minutes or until the onion has turned slightly clear, and the vegetables are a little soft.

Now add the broth and herbs, stir well, and turn the heat to high. Allow the broth to boil, and then reduce the heat to a simmer. Cook for 5 minutes. Now add the carrot and chicken, and cook for about 5 minutes. Add the zucchini, and cook for a few more minutes. Serve once the noodles are soft.

Italian Sausage Stew With Zucchini Noodles

Serves: 4

Ingredients:
10 ounces Italian turkey sausage (Casings removed)
Salt & pepper
1 tsp olive oil
½ tsp olive oil
1 zucchini
4 cups chicken stock
1 can diced tomatoes
¼ onion (Chopped)
1 tbsp tomato paste
¼ green bell pepper (Chopped)
½ tbsp oregano
¼ red bell pepper (Chopped)
1 tsp fennel
½ tbsp cilantro

Method
Spiralize the zucchini to create ribbon-shaped noodles. Now heat 1 tsp olive oil in a pan, and add the sausages. Cook for about 10 minutes, or until the sausage has browned and there's no liquid in the pan. Once the sausage is done, transfer it to a soup pot, and add the tomato paste, chicken stock, diced tomatoes, basil, fennel, oregano and cilantro, and simmer.

Add the peppers and onion along with the remaining olive oil to a pan, and cook for 2-3 minutes, then add to the pot. Stir well. Allow to simmer for about 45 minutes, and then add the noodles. Season, stir, and cook for another 20 minutes, or until the noodles have reached your desired consistency. Serve.

Zucchini & Rosemary Soup

Serves: 4

Ingredients:
1 tbsp butter
2 zucchinis
½ tbsp vegetable oil
1 potato (Peeled, sliced)
½ onion (Chopped)
2 cups chicken broth
1 cup rosemary (Minced)
2 garlic cloves (Sliced)

Method
Spiralize the zucchini to create ribbons. Heat the butter in a pan on a medium-high heat. Add the onion and sauté for a few minutes until it's translucent. Add the rosemary and garlic, and stir well. Now pour in the broth, and add the potatoes. Allow the contents of the pan to come to the boil, and then reduce the heat. Allow to simmer for 10 minutes, and then add the zucchini ribbons. Stir, and cook for about 10-15 minutes, depending on your preferred texture. Sprinkle the green onions on top of the soup and serve.

White Bean Soup With Zucchini Ribbons

Serves: 6

Ingredients:
2 cups white beans
½ cup cilantro (Fresh)
6 cups chicken stock
1 tsp hot pepper flakes
½ cup onion (Chopped)
Black pepper
1 tsp cilantro (Dried)
½ zucchini
1 tsp marjoram
16 ounces Italian turkey sausage
1 tsp fennel
1 tsp garlic (minced)

Method

Spiralize the zucchini to create thin noodles, and set to one side. Add the beans to a pot, and pour in the chicken stock. Now add the basil, onion, fennel, marjoram, cilantro, garlic, and onion, stir well, and cook on a low heat for about 1 hour, or until the beans are slightly tender.

Now preheat your oven to 400 Fahrenheit, and roast the sausages until they're a little brown. This should take about 25 minutes. Remove the sausages from the pan, deglaze it using water, then add the water to the soup. Halve the sausages, and add the pieces to the soup. Simmer, adding a little water is the soup is thickening. Now add the zucchini to the beans along with the pepper flakes, and black pepper. Simmer for about 20 minutes. Once the beans are completely soft, add the cilantro and cook for a few more minutes. Serve.

Kohrabi & Carrot Soup

Serves: 3

Ingredients:
3 carrots
1 cm ginger
1 kohlrabi
Salt & pepper
1 onion (Chopped)
½ cup parsley (Chopped)
100g cream cheese
Small slice butter
2 cups vegetable stock

Method
Spiralize the carrot and kohlrabi to create thick noodles. Add the butter to a pot and simmer on a low heat. Add the noodles and stock, and cook on a medium heat for 10-15 minutes. Lower the heat and add the parsley, cheese, and salt & pepper. Stir. Cook for 5 more minutes, and spoon the soup into bowls. Sprinkle with the parsley, and serve.

Chicken Sausage Soup With Zucchini Noodles

Serves: 4

Ingredients:
1 tbsp olive oil
2 zucchinis
4 chicken sausages (Casing removed)
6 cups chicken broth
¼ tsp red pepper flakes
Salt & pepper
2 cloves garlic (Minced)
2 celery stalks (Diced)
½ red onion (Diced)
1 tbsp pine nuts
1 garlic clove (Chopped)
2 cups cilantro
1 tbsp olive oil
2 tbsp Parmesan

Method
Spiralize the zucchini to make ribbons, set to one side.
Add the olive oil to a soup pot, and heat it on a
medium-high heat. Then add the sausage, and
crumble it. Cook for about 5 minutes or until it starts
to brown. Add the 2 cloves garlic, celery, red pepper
flakes and onion, and season. Cook for about 3
minutes. Now add the broth, and bring it to the boil.
Allow to cook for 5 minutes, and then add the zucchini
ribbons, and cook for 5 minutes, or until the ribbons'
texture is per your preferences.

Once the ribbons are done add the pine nuts, single garlic clove, cilantro, olive oil, and Parmesan to a food processor, and pulse for 30 seconds.
Once the soup is cooked to your satisfaction, spoon it into a bowl and top with the pesto. Serve.

Sausage & Kale Soup With Carrot Noodles

Serves: 2

Ingredients:
175 grams sweet Italian sausage (Casings removed)
½ tsp red pepper flakes
1 garlic clove (Minced)
1 carrot (Peeled)
¼ cup onions (Diced)
½ tsp oregano
Salt & pepper
3 cups chicken broth
2 cups curly kale (Chopped)

Method
Spiralize the carrot to create thin noodles, and set to one side. Add the sausage to a pot on a medium-high heat, and crumble it using a spoon. Cook the sausage for about 10 minutes, or until it's browned nicely. Add the onions and garlic, and then season and stir. Cook for about 3-4 minutes, or until the onions are soft.

Now add the kale and cook for 1 minute. Stir well. Add the oregano and chicken broth and increase the heat to high. Allow to boil, and then add the carrots and stir well. Turn the heat to low, and allow to cook for 5 minutes. Spoon the soup into bowls and garnish with the red pepper flakes. Serve.

Beef Stew & Zucchini Noodles
Serves: 4

Ingredients
1 pound beef stew chunks
¼ cup parsley (Chopped)
½ red onion (Diced)
4 zucchinis
¼ tsp red pepper flakes
2 bay leaves
2 garlic cloves (Minced)
4 cups beef broth
3 celery stalks (Diced)
14 ounces tomatoes (Diced)
3 carrots (Peeled, diced)
Salt & pepper
3 tbsp Worcestershire sauce
½ tsp cayenne pepper
1 tsp thyme

Method
Spiralize the zucchini into ribbons and set to one side.
Place a pan on a medium heat and add the olive oil
allow to heat slightly and then add the beef. Cook the
beef for 8-10 minutes or until it's browned. Spoon the
beef out of the pan, and set to one side.

Add the garlic to the beef juices and cook for 30
seconds. Now add the red pepper flakes and onions,
and cook for a minute. Add the carrots and celery, stir,
and cook for 2 minutes. Add the beef back to the pan,

and sprinkle in the cayenne pepper and thyme, stir, and add the Worcestershire sauce. Stir again. Season, stir, and add the tomatoes and broth. Stir again, and add the bay leaves. Cover, and bring to the boil.

Reduce the heat to a simmer, and cook for 40 minutes. Take the lid off the pan and simmer for about 30 minutes, or until the stew is thick. Spoon the soup and noodles into bowls, and sprinkle the parsley on top. Serve.

Thai-Style Papaya Salad

Serves: 4

Ingredients

1 green papaya (Peeled, halved, de-seeded)
4 tbsp peanuts (Roasted)
6 red chilis
4 vine tomatoes (Sliced)
4 cloves garlic (Peeled)
4 tbsp fish sauce
1 cup green beans (Chopped)
Juice of 2 limes

Method

Spiralize the papaya to create ribbons, and set to one side. Add the garlic, and chili to a bowl, and mash them together well. Add the beans and peanuts mash a little. Now pour in the lime juice and fish sauce, and toss well. Take a bowl, and add the tomatoes and ribbons, pour the fish sauce mix over the top, and stir well. Serve.

Bell Pepper & Artichoke Salad

Serves: 2

Ingredients
½ red bell pepper
¾ tsp oregano
½ orange bell pepper
Salt & pepper
¾ cup artichokes (Quartered)
1 tsp olive oil
1/8 cup provolone cheese
1 cup mixed greens
½ cup black olives (Halved)
1 tbsp cilantro (Chopped)

Method
Spiralize the bell peppers to create thin noodles.

Preheat your oven to 450 Fahrenheit, and line 2 baking sheets with some parchment. Add the noodles to one of the baking sheets, and lay them out. Season, and add the oregano. Set to one side.

Add the artichokes to a bowl, and then add the olive oil, garlic powder and a bit of salt & pepper. Stir well. Now spread the artichoke mix onto the other baking sheet.

Add both baking sheets to the oven and cook for about 20 minutes. When the ingredients are cooked, add them to a bowl, along with the cheese, cilantro, and olives. Toss well, sprinkle on the mixed greens, and serve.

Mozzarella & Cashew Nut Zucchini Noodle Salad

Serves: 2

Ingredients
¼ cup cashews (Soaked)
1 tsp Dijon mustard
1 tbsp balsamic vinegar
Salt & pepper
¼ cup cashew milk
1 clove garlic (Pressed)
½ cup mozzarella pearls
1 tbsp pine nuts
1 cup cherry tomatoes (Halved)
1 zucchini
1 orange bell pepper

Method
Spiralize the zucchini to create thin noodles and the bell pepper to create thicker noodles, and set to one side. Add the cashews, vinegar, garlic, milk, mustard, and some seasoning to a blender, and blend until the dressing is creamy. Add the tomatoes, bell pepper, and mozzarella to a bowl and mix well. Drizzle the dressing over the salad, and then add the salad to the refrigerator.

Take a skillet, and add the pine nuts, toast them on a medium heat for about 5 minutes or until they are a golden color. Now remove the salad from the refrigerator, and spoon it into bowls. Sprinkle the pine nuts on top, and serve.

Goats Cheese Salad With Cucumbers

Serves: 4

Ingredients
1 tsp olive oil
Salt & pepper
3 pieces' whole wheat bread
1 cucumber
3 tbsp olive oil
3 tbsp mint (Chopped)
Pinch red pepper flakes
4 cilantro leaves (Sliced)
2 tsp red wine vinegar
1 cup cherry tomatoes (Halved)
2/3 cup pitted green olives (Quartered)
3 ounces goats cheese (Crumbled)
1 garlic clove (Minced)

Method
Spiralize the cucumber to create ribbons. Heat a
skillet on a medium-high heat, and add the olive oil.
As soon as the oil is heated, add the bread and cook
for 3 minutes. Turn the slices over, season, and cook
for another 3 minutes, or until the bread is a golden
brown color. Remove the bread from the skillet, and
chop it into cubes.

Now add the cucumber, cheese, red wine vinegar,
olives, cilantro, and mint to a bowl, and stir well.
Season, and then add the bread and toss well. Serve.

Spiralized Mixed Vegetable Salad
Serves: 2

Ingredients:
4 carrots
Sesame seeds
1 zucchini
Ground pepper
1 yellow squash
¼ cup olive oil
¼ cup Greek yogurt
¾ tsp salt
½ avocado
1 garlic clove (Minced)
¼ cup water
½ cup cilantro
2 tbsp lemon zest & juice
15 ounces chickpeas
2 tbsp olive oil

Method
Spiralize the zucchini, carrots and squash, and create different thicknesses of noodles. Set to one side. Preheat your oven to 400 Fahrenheit, and pat the chickpeas dry. Now add them to a bowl with ½ tsp salt, and 2 tbsp oil. Add to the oven, and roast for 30 minutes, or until they are crispy.

Add the spiralized vegetables to a bowl, and mix. Now add the avocado, water, yogurt, garlic, the rest of the salt, and the cilantro, lemon juice and zest, to a blender, and blend until smooth. Add the dressing to the noodles, and then sprinkle the sesame seeds and chickpeas on top. Serve.

Rainbow Noodle Crunch With Chili & Lime Vinaigrette

Serves: 2

Ingredients:
1 orange bell pepper
1 tbsp toasted sesame oil
1 cup purple cabbage
2 tbsp rice vinegar
1 carrot
2 tbsp grapeseed oil
1 radish
1 tbsp black sesame seeds
1 cup cilantro
4 ounces bean thread noodles
1 tsp ginger
3 tbsp tamari
1 red bell pepper
1 tsp maple syrup
3 scallions (Chopped)
2 tbsp lime juice
1 tbsp chili & garlic sauce

Method
Spiralize the radish, peppers, carrots and cabbage to create noodles, and set to one side. Add the tamari, rice vinegar, lime juice, grapeseed oil, chili-garlic sauce, sesame oil, ginger root and maple syrup to a bowl, and whisk well. Set to one side.

Take a large bowl, add the bean noodles, and pour enough hot water over them to cover them completely. Stand for 15 minutes. Add the vegetable noodles to a bowl and pour the dressing over the top. Add the noodles, toss well, and sprinkle the black sesame seeds on top. Serve.

Casseroles

Mexican Style Sweet Potato Casserole
Serves: 4-6

Ingredients
1 pound cooked chicken breast (Boneless, skinless, shredded)
5 ounces pepper jack cheese (Shredded)
2 sweet potatoes
1 can black beans (Drained)
4 vine tomatoes
1 cup corn (Frozen)
2 guajillo chili peppers (Dried)
1 ¼ tsp salt
1 tsp olive oil
½ tsp cumin
1 onion (Quartered)
4 garlic cloves

Method
Spiralize the potatoes to create small noodles, and add them to a casserole dish. Preheat your oven to 400 Fahrenheit. Now add some water to a large pot, and bring it to the boil., Add the peppers, and cover. Simmer for about 10 -15 minutes, or until the peppers are a little soft. Remove from the pot, and allow to cool. Stem the peppers and remove the seeds. Once you've removed the seeds, add the peppers to a blender. Place the tomatoes in the water you cooked

the peppers in, and allow to cook for 10 minutes. Once the potatoes are done, take them out of the pan, and peel the skin away.

Add the potatoes to the blender, and blend until you have a smooth mixture. In a skillet, add the onion and garlic, and sauté then until they're brown. Now add the onion and garlic to the blender, sprinkle in the salt, pepper and cumin, and blend once more.

Once you've blended all the ingredients together, pour this mixture into a bowl, add the black beans, chicken, and corn, and mix well. Add the potatoes, and mix again. Top with the cheese, and cover the casserole with foil. Add to the oven and bake for 1 hour, or until the potato noodles are tender. Serve.

Zucchini And Artichoke Casserole
Serves: 3-4

Ingredients
2 zucchinis
¾ cup Parmesan (Shredded)
Salt & pepper
7 ounces artichokes
1/3 cup egg whites
1 ½ cups spinach (Chopped)
2 eggs
1/8 cup cilantro (Chopped)
1 tbsp cilantro (Chopped)
½ tbsp garlic (Minced)
½ tsp garlic (Minced)
¼ cup roasted red peppers (Sliced)
1/8 cup red onion (Chopped)1/4 cup Greek yogurt

Method
Spiralize the zucchini to make thin noodles, and set to one side. Preheat your oven to 350 Fahrenheit, and then spray some cooking spray onto a skillet. Add the noodles to a colander and sprinkle with some salt. Allow to stand for 15-20 minutes while tossing occasionally.

Add 1/8 tsp salt, cilantro, red peppers, eggs, garlic, red onion, yogurt and a sprinkle of pepper to a blender, and blend until smooth. Once the mixture is smooth, add it to a bowl.

Squeeze the moisture out of the zucchini, and lay them on a paper towel, and allow the moisture to be soaked up. Once the moisture has been soaked up, add the zucchini noodles to the red pepper mix.

Now add the artichokes, spinach, and ½ the Parmesan to the mix, and toss well. Now add the mixture to a casserole dish, and press it down until the mixture is flat. Sprinkle the rest of the Parmesan on top, and bake for about 45 minutes, or until the casserole is set. Once the casserole is set, turn on your broiler, and broil on a high heat for 3 minutes, or until the top of the casserole is a nice golden brown. Allow to cool for 20-30 minutes, and serve.

Sweet Potato Spaghetti Casserole

Serves: 4

Ingredients

2 sweet potatoes (Peeled)
4 cilantro leaves
2 ounces cream cheese
5 ounces feta cheese
2/3 cup almond milk
1 cup spinach leaves
1 egg
2/3 cup sausage (Cooked)
1 egg white
¼ cup tomato sauce
1 tbsp oil
2 ounces pimento (Diced)
½ tsp garlic (Minced)
¼ tsp onion salt

Method

Spiralize the sweet potato to create thin noodles, and set them to one side. Preheat your oven to 350 Fahrenheit. Now take the noodles and add them to a bowl, place them in the microwave for 1 minute to steam them. Remove from the microwave, and add the onion salt and garlic, along with the oil. Toss so the noodles become coated in the oil.

Add the milk, eggs and cream cheese to a different bowl, stir well, and then spray some cooking oil onto a casserole dish.

Add the noodles, to the casserole dish, then layer on the sausage, spinach, cream cheese mix, tomato sauce, and feta. Add the casserole to the oven, and cook for 30-35 minutes, or until the cheese starts to go a little brown. Once the casserole is done, remove it from the oven, sprinkle the cilantro, and serve.

Sweet Potato And Pecan Casserole
Serves: 5-6

Ingredients
2 sweet potatoes (Peeled)
¼ tsp cinnamon
1 tbsp butter (Melted)
½ tbsp coconut sugar
1 ½ tbsp maple syrup
¾ cup raw pecans
1/3 cup powdered sugar
½ can coconut cream

Method
Spiralize the potatoes to create thin noodles. Preheat your oven to 375 Fahrenheit, and add the noodles, cinnamon, sugar, maple syrup and butter to a bowl, and stir. Now add the noodles to a dish, and place it in the oven for 10 minutes, or until the noodles are soft. Once the noodles are soft, turn your broiler to 400 Fahrenheit, and cook the noodles for another 10 minutes.

Now take the pecans and add them to a skillet, and cook them for 5 minutes. Add 1 tbsp maple syrup, and cook for another 5 minutes. Stir until the syrup has crystallized, then remove them from the heat.

Take the coconut cream, and add the top layer to a mixing bowl. Beat the cream until it becomes whipped, and add the sugar. Whip a little more, and then add the rest of the coconut cream. Whip again until the cream has the same consistency as a salad dressing.

Now take the noodles, and pour the coconut cream over them, sprinkle the pecans on, and serve.

BBQ Chicken And Zucchini Noodle Casserole
Serves: 4

Ingredients
4 zucchinis
Salt & pepper
½ cup plain Greek yogurt
½ cup cilantro (Chopped)
½ cup BBQ sauce
1 cup chicken breast (Shredded)
1 ½ cups cheddar cheese (Shredded)

Method
Spiralize the zucchini to create your desired thickness
of noodles, and set to one side. Preheat your oven to
200 Fahrenheit, and line two baking sheets with some
paper towels. Now divide the noodles between both
baking sheets, and sprinkle with salt. Add the noodles
to the oven, and bake for 40 minutes, so they dry a
little. After the 40 minutes is up, remove the noodles
from the oven, and add them to some more paper
towels, and allow any extra moisture to drain away.

Now turn your oven up to 375 Fahrenheit, and add the
BBQ sauce, yogurt, and half of the cheese to a pan, on
a medium-high heat. Cook the ingredients until the
cheese starts to melt, this should take about 10
minutes.

Once the cheese has melted, quickly add the chicken,
noodles and cilantro to a bowl. Stir well, and cut it up

as you do so. Pour the melted cheese over the noodles, and add a pinch of pepper. Mix well, and then add the mixture to a casserole dish. Spread evenly, and cook for 20 minutes, then top with the rest of the cheese, and place it back in the oven for another 20 minutes, or until the cheese starts to bubble.

Remove the casserole from the oven, and allow it to cool, then pour the BBQ sauce over the top. Serve.

Enchilada Sweet Potato Casserole

Serves: 6

Ingredients
2 cups chicken (Cooked, shredded)
Parsley
2 cups red enchilada sauce
½ avocado (Chopped)
15 ounces black beans (Drained)
1 green onion (Chopped)
15 ounces corn (Drained)
6 ounces Colby jack cheese (Shredded)
Salt & pepper
2 sweet potatoes

Method
Spiralize your sweet potatoes to create some spaghetti noodles, and set to one side. Preheat your oven to 400 Fahrenheit, and then add the enchilada sauce, corn, black beans, and chicken to a bowl, mix well, and then season and set to one side.

Now spray a casserole dish with cooking spray, and add the sweet potato noodles. Pour the chicken mix over the noodles, and then sprinkle the cheese on top. Cover with foil, and add to the oven for 1 hour, or until the cheese is bubbling. Remove the foil for the last 10 minutes. Allow the casserole to stand for a few minutes, and top with the avocado, green onions, and parsley. Serve.

Brussels Sprouts & Potato Noodle Casserole
Serves: 2-3

Ingredients
4 Brussels sprouts (Chopped lengthwise)
¾ cup cheddar cheese (Shredded)
3 bacon strips
1 Idaho potato (Peeled)
1 garlic clove (Minced)
¼ cup red onion (Diced)
Pinch red pepper flakes

Method
Spiralize the potato to create thick noodles, and set to one side. Add the bacon to a skillet, and cook on a medium heat until the bacon is crispy (This should take about 5 minutes). Drain all the bacon grease apart from ½ tbsp from the skillet. Add the garlic to the skillet, and cook for 30 seconds, add the onions and red pepper flakes, and cook for 2 minutes. Now add the Brussels sprouts, and cook for 3 minutes.

Stir in the noodles, and toss well. Add the bacon and crumble it. Now let the noodles cook for about 2 minutes. Cover, and then cook for another 3 minutes. Stir, and cook for 3 more minutes, or until the noodles are slightly browned, and thoroughly cooked. Add the noodle mix to a casserole dish, sprinkle the cheese on top, and serve.

Tex-Mex Chicken And Sweet Potato Casserole

Serves: 2-3

Ingredients
1 cup chicken (Cooked, shredded)
½ cup mozzarella (Shredded)
8 ounces black beans
1 tsp taco seasoning
1 sweet potato
¼ tsp pepper
1 tbsp olive oil
¼ tsp salt
½ onion (Chopped)
½ tsp cumin
1 ½ garlic cloves (Peeled)
1 tomato (Chopped)
½ Jalapeño (Quartered)

Method
Spiralize the potato to create fine noodles, and add them to a casserole dish.

Heat a pan on a high heat, and add the oil, garlic, and onion. Cook for 2 minutes, or until the onions are turning brown. Add the Jalapeño, tomatoes, and all the spices, stir, and cook for another 2 minutes, or until the tomatoes are soft. Now add everything to a blender, and blend until everything is mixed well, and looking like salsa.

Take a bowl, and add the salsa, black beans and chicken, stir well. Now pour the salsa on top of the potato noodles, and cover with the cheese. Add the casserole to the oven, and cook for 35 minutes, or until the cheese is melted. Serve.

Asparagus & Cheese Potato Noodle Casserole
Serves: 4

Ingredients
1 large potato
1 tsp Parmesan (Shredded)
1 cup Gruyère cheese (Shredded)
Pepper
5 asparagus spears

Method
Spiralize the potato to make ribbons, and set to one side. Now preheat your oven to 400 Fahrenheit, sprinkle on half of the Gruyère, and add the ribbons to the dish. Spread the rest of the Gruyère on top, and add the asparagus on top of that. Sprinkle some black pepper on top, and then place the casserole in the oven for 30 minutes.

Remove the dish from the oven, and set it to broil. Add the Parmesan on top, and place the dish under the broiler for 2 minutes. Slice, and serve.

Cheesy Zucchini Noodle Casserole
Serves: 5-6

Ingredients
5 zucchinis
½ cup Parmesan (Shredded)
4 ½ tsp salt
2 cups mozzarella (Shredded)
1 tbsp olive oil
¾ ricotta cheese
8 ounces Italian sausage (Casings removed)
1 ½ cups onion (Diced)
½ cup cilantro leaves (Sliced)
3 cloves garlic (minced)
15 ounces crushed tomatoes

Method
Spiralize the zucchini to create thin noodles, then toss with some salt and allow the zucchini to drain. Now beak up the sausage and brown it in a pan coated with the olive oil, on a medium heat. Once the sausage is a little brown, remove it from the pan, and discard all of the fat, apart from 1 tbsp.

Now add the garlic and onions to the pan, and cook for about 5 minutes, or until they have softened a little. Add the sausage, tomatoes and cilantro, and simmer. Cook for 5 minutes, and then add the salt, and stir. Now add the noodles, and stir well, then transfer everything to a casserole dish, and top with the Parmesan and Mozzarella. Bake in the oven for 35 minutes at 350 Fahrenheit, or until the cheese is bubbling. Allow to cool for at least 5 minutes, and then serve.

Tuna & Zucchini Casserole
Serves: 6

Ingredients
1 ½ tsp olive oil
¼ tsp garlic powder
2 garlic cloves (Minced)
¼ tsp parsley flakes
¼ tsp red pepper flakes
¼ tsp cilantro flakes
1 white onion (Diced)
1 tsp oregano flakes
3 celery stalks (Diced)
1 tbsp water
½ cup almond meal
8 ounces baby mushrooms (Chopped)
3 zucchinis
½ tsp thyme flakes
15 ounces tuna in water (Drained)
Salt & pepper
½ cup chicken broth
1/3 cup Parmesan (Shredded)

Method
Spiralize the zucchinis to create ribbons, and set to one side. Preheat your oven to 375 Fahrenheit, and spray a casserole dish with cooking spray. Now take a pot and place it on a medium heat. Add the olive oil, and then the red pepper flakes and garlic. Cook for about 30 seconds, and then add the onions, cook for a few more minutes before adding the mushrooms and

celery. Stir, add the oregano, salt, pepper, and thyme, and stir again.

Cook for 2-3 minutes, and then add the broth and cook until the broth has reduced down to half, and then add the Parmesan, and stir well.

Now place the almond meal, ¼ tsp oregano, cilantro, parsley, and garlic into a bowl. Season, add the water, and using your fingers, roll the ingredients until a dough is formed. Set to one side.

Add the tuna to the broth, and cook for 1 minute, and then pour the ingredients into a casserole dish. Add the noodles, and toss a little to combine. Take the almond meal, and crumble it over the casserole. Cover, and bake for about 20 minutes. Remove the cover, and bake for another 10 minutes, or until the breadcrumbs are a little brown. Remove from the oven, drain away any excess water, and serve.

Broccoli & Cheese Zoodle Casserole
Serves: 4

Ingredients
2 zucchinis
¾ cup cheddar cheese (Shredded)
Salt & pepper
1 cup kale (Torn)
2 eggs
1 cup broccoli (Chopped)
½ cup egg whites
¼ cup plain Greek yogurt

Method
Spiralize the zucchini so it creates thick noodles, and set to one side. Preheat your oven to 350 Fahrenheit, and spray some cooking spray onto a skillet, and set to one side.

Place the zucchini into a colander, and sprinkle with some salt. Allow to sit for about 15-20 minutes so the moisture is absorbed. Take the egg whites and add them to a bowl, now stir in the pepper and Greek yogurt, and then whisk until smooth. Add the noodles to some paper towels to further absorb any moisture, and then add them to a bowl along with the broccoli, ¼ cup cheddar and egg mix. Stir well, and pour this mixture into the skillet, and make sure you spread it evenly.

Sprinkle the rest of the cheese on top, and then cook for about 40 minutes, or until the eggs come away from the sides of the skillet.

Now switch the oven on to a high broil, and broil the casserole for 2 minutes, or until the eggs are starting to go a little brown. Serve.

One-Pot Taco Zucchini Noodle Casserole
Serves: 6

Ingredients
1 pound ground turkey
1 avocado (Sliced)
14 ounces tomato sauce
4 zucchinis
2 tbsp tomato paste
1 cup cherry tomatoes (Halved)
2 tbsp chili powder
1 cup cheddar (Shredded)
2 tbsp cumin
1 cup corn kernels
1 tsp onion powder
14 ounces black beans (Drained)
1 tsp garlic powder
¼ tsp pepper
¼ tsp paprika
¼ tsp salt
1/8 tsp cayenne pepper

Method
Spiralize the zucchinis to create ribbons, and then place them into a colander, and sprinkle with some salt. Allow to sit for about 15-20 minutes so the moisture is absorbed. Add the noodles to some paper towels to further absorb any moisture.

Heat a skillet on a medium-high heat, and spray with cooking spray. Add the turkey and cook for about 3 minutes, or until it's browned. Add the cayenne pepper, tomato paste, tomato sauce, garlic powder, onion powder, paprika, salt, pepper and cumin, and mix well. Cook for 3 minutes, or until the sauce starts to thicken. Then add the cheese, beans, cherry tomatoes, and corn, stir again, and cook for 2 minutes, or until the ingredients have heated through.

Add the noodles to the skillet, and cook for about 5 minutes. Then remove from the heat, and add the avocado. Serve.

Ground Turkey With Zoodles & Pesto
Serves: 6

Ingredients:
3 ½ pounds zucchinis
Red pepper flakes
3 tbsp olive oil
½ cup Parmesan (Shredded)
1 red onion (Minced)
Salt & pepper
2 garlic cloves (Minced)
¼ cup pesto
4 ounces mushrooms (Sliced)
3 tbsp tomato paste
1 pound ground turkey

Method
Spiralize your zucchini to make thin noodles, and set to one side. Add 1 tbsp olive oil to a skillet and heat on a medium-high heat. When then oil is hot, add the noodles, and cook until they are tender, this should only take a few minutes. Sprinkle with salt & pepper, and set to one side.

Now add the rest of the olive oil, along with the mushrooms, onions, and garlic, and cook for a few minutes until the onions are translucent, then set them to one side. Now add the turkey to the skillet, and cook for about 5 minutes, or until the turkey is light brown. Season, and then add the tomato paste, pesto, and mix well. Add the mushroom mix to the meat, and stir, and heat for about 2-3 minutes. Now place the meat onto a plate, add the zoodles on top, and sprinkle the cheese and red pepper flakes on top. Serve.

Zucchini Pizza Casserole
Serves: 4-6

Ingredients:
2 zucchinis
½ cup extra sharp cheddar
½ tsp salt
1 cup Mozzarella
2 eggs
8 ounces mushrooms (Sliced)
1/8 cup Parmesan cheese
1 bell pepper (Diced)
½ tsp Italian seasoning
2 cups spaghetti sauce
½ pound ground beef
2 tbsp onion powder

Method
Spiralize the zucchini to make thin noodles, and then place them into a colander, and sprinkle with some salt. Allow to sit for about 15-20 minutes so the moisture is absorbed. Add the noodles to some paper towels to further absorb any moisture.

Add the zucchini and eggs to a bowl, along with all of the Parmesan, ¼ cup Mozzarella, and ¼ cup cheddar, stir well, then add the Italian seasoning. Now add the zucchini mix to a baking dish, and press it down well. Bake for about 20 minutes in an oven that's been preheated to 400 Fahrenheit.

While the zucchini is cooking, add the beef to a skillet, and cook for about 10 minutes on a medium heat, or until the meat is cooked through. Drain away any grease, and then add the onion and spaghetti sauce.

Once the zucchini is done, remove it from the oven, and then add the meat mix on top. Spread evenly, and then add the peppers and mushrooms. Sprinkle the rest of the cheese on top, and add the pizza casserole to the oven. Cook for about 20 minutes, or until the cheese is melted and a little brown. Remove the dish from the oven, and stand for a few minutes. Serve.

Rice Dishes

Butternut Squash Rice With Sausage & Stuffing
Serves: 6

Ingredients
1 butternut squash
½ cup Parmesan (Shredded)
1 tbsp olive oil
Salt & pepper
3 garlic cloves (Minced)
3 celery stalks (Diced)
2 tbsp parsley (Chopped)
½ cup yellow onion (Diced)
1 gala apple
2 tsp thyme
¾ cup pecans (Chopped)
3 Italian sausages (Casings removed)

Method
Spiralize the butternut squash to create short, thin noodles. Then spiralize the apple to create thick noodles. Preheat your oven to 400 Fahrenheit. Add the butternut squash to a food processor, and blend well until it looks like rice. Set to one side. Now take a skillet, and place it on a medium heat. Add the olive oil, and once it's heated, add the onion, garlic, thyme and celery. Season and stir, and cook for about 5

minutes, or until the vegetables are starting to go a little soft.

Add the sausages and break them up a little. Cook until the sausages aren't pink in the middle. This should take about 5 minutes. Now add the rice, parsley, and apples, season and stir. Cook for another 2 minutes, or until everything is heated thoroughly. Transfer the contents of the skillet to a casserole dish, and add the pecans. Stir well, and sprinkle the Parmesan on top. Place the casserole dish in your oven, and cook for 15 minutes, or until the rice is soft. Serve.

Roasted Carrot Rice
Serves: 2

<u>Ingredients</u>
4 carrots
Cooking spray
Salt & pepper

<u>Method</u>
Spiralize the carrots to create short, thin noodles, and then place the carrot noodles in a food processor. Blend until the noodles look like rice.

Preheat your oven to 350 Fahrenheit, and line a baking sheet with parchment. Now place the carrot rice on the baking sheet, and make sure you spread them evenly. Season, and spray the cooking oil on the top of the carrots. Bake in the oven for about 15-20 minutes, or until the edges of the carrot rice are turning a little brown. Serve.

Squash Risotto With Parmesan And Asparagus
Serves: 4

Ingredients
1 butternut squash
½ cup green peas (Cooked)
1 tbsp olive oil
½ cup Parmesan (Shredded)
Cooking spray
1 cup vegetable broth
2 tbsp vegetable broth
6 asparagus stalks (Chopped into thirds)
¼ cup red onion (Diced)
Salt & pepper

Method
Spiralize the butternut squash to create short, thin noodles, and then add it to a food processor. Pulse until the noodles are rice-shaped, and set to one side. Now heat some cooking spray in a skillet on a medium heat, and add the asparagus. Season, and cook for a few minutes, or until the asparagus is soft and bright green. Set to one side.

Now take another skillet, and heat the olive oil on a medium-low heat. Add the garlic, cook for 30 seconds, and add the onion. Allow the onion to soften, and then add 2 tbsp vegetable broth. Cook until the broth has reduced (About 10 minutes), and then add ½ cup of the broth. Reduce again, and then add the other ½ cup. This should take 15-20 minutes. One the rice is cooked to your satisfaction, add the Parmesan, stir well, and cook for up to 30 seconds, or until the cheese is melted.

Add the peas and asparagus to the risotto, stir well, and serve.

Sweet Potato Rice With Vegetarian Chili
Serves: 2-3

Ingredients
½ sweet potato
2 avocados
1 garlic clove (minced)
1 tbsp parsley (Chopped)
1/3 cup red onion (Diced)
7 ounces red kidney beans
1 tbsp olive oil
7 ounces white beans
½ cup celery (Diced)
7 ounces diced tomatoes
½ cup carrots (Diced)
1 cup water
½ cup red bell pepper (Diced)
1 cup vegetable broth
½ tsp cumin
Salt & pepper
½ tsp oregano
¼ tsp chili powder

Method
Spiralize the sweet potatoes to create thin noodles, then add them to a food processor and pulse until they are rice-like. Set to one side. Take a pot and place it on a medium heat. Add the olive oil and allow to heat, once heat, add the garlic and cook for about 30 seconds. Add the onions and cook for about 2 minutes, or until they are translucent. Add the

peppers, carrots, and celery and stir. Now add the salt & pepper, chili powder, oregano, and cumin, stir again, and cook for another 5 minutes.

Pour in the broth, as well as the beans, tomatoes and water, cover and bring the heat to a boil. As soon as the mixture is boiling, remove the cover, and reduce to a simmer. Add the parsley, stir, and cook for 20 minutes. Now add the rice, stir well, and cook for another 10 minutes. Serve.

Stuffed Plantain Rice Balls With Goat Cheese
Serves: 6

Ingredients
2 plantains (Peeled)
5 tsp goat cheese
1 slice whole wheat toast
3 tsp coconut flakes
Salt
1 egg (Beaten)

Method
Spiralize the plantains to make noodles, then add them to a food processor. Pulse so the noodles become rice-like, and set to one side. Preheat your oven to 400 Fahrenheit. Now add the toast to the food processor and pulse to turn it into breadcrumbs. Set to one side.

Take a skillet and add some cooking spray, heat on a medium heat, and add the rice. Stir and toast until the rice is starting to brown, this should take 5-10 minutes. Once the rice is done, add it to a bowl, then sprinkle in the breadcrumbs, coconut, salt, and egg. Stir well and set to one side. Take a baking sheet, line with parchment, and then scoop some of the rice mix into your hands. Make approximately 6 rice balls and place them on the baking sheet. Now take some goat cheese, roll that into 6 balls, and stuff those balls into the rice balls. Re-shape the rice balls, and place them back on the baking sheet. Add to the oven, cook for 15 minutes, and serve.

Slow Cooked Coconut Chicken Curry With Turnip Rice

Serves: 4

Ingredients:
4 chicken breasts (Boneless, skinless)
¼ cup cilantro
1 red chili pepper (Chopped)
Salt & pepper
5 ounces green beans (Trimmed)
1 tsp ginger (Minced)
3 garlic cloves (Minced)
½ white onion (Chopped)
2 tsp coconut oil
14 ounces coconut milk
2 turnips
1 tsp turmeric
½ cup cashews
2 tbsp curry powder

Method
Spiralize the turnips to make noodles, then add them to a food processor. Pulse so the noodles become rice-like. Set to one side. Add the chicken, 2 cloves garlic, red peppers and onions to your slow cooker. Take a bowl and add the turmeric, salt & pepper, coconut milk, and curry powder. Stir well, and pour this mixture into the slow cooker, ensuring the chicken is covered. Cook for 2 ½ to 3 hours on a high heat, and then add the cashews. Cook for 15 more minutes.

Now add some oil to a skillet, and turn the heat up to medium-high. As soon as the oil starts to heat up, add the ginger and remaining clove of garlic, and cook for 1 minute. Add the rice, season, stir well, and cook for 7 minutes, or until the rice is cooked to your satisfaction. Remove from the heat, add the cilantro, and place on plates to serve. Top with the chicken, green beans and onions, and pour the sauce over the top. Serve.

Miso Beet Rice With Egg

Serves: 2

Ingredients:
1 tbsp miso
2 eggs
2 tbsp rice vinegar
2 scallions (Diced)
½ tsp ginger (Grated)
2 cups spinach
1 tbsp sesame oil
1 beet
½ tbsp honey
1 tbsp water

Method
Spiralize the beet to make noodles, then add them to a food processor. Pulse so the noodles become rice-like. Set to one side. Add the miso, rice vinegar, sesame oil, ginger, water and honey to a bowl, stir well, and set to one side.

Take a skillet, and cook the spinach in it on a medium heat for 5 minutes, or until it's wilted. Now add the spinach to the bowl of dressing, and toss well. Add the eggs to the same skillet, and cook until they are done as per your preferences. Now spoon the rice onto plates, add the eggs on top, and then pour a bit of the dressing over each plate of rice. Sprinkle the sesame seeds and scallions on top, and serve.

Maple Pecan Pork With Sweet Potato Risotto & Goat Cheese

Serves: 4

Ingredients:
4 pork chops (Boneless)
1 tsp chili powder
Salt & pepper
½ cup pecans (Very crushed)
2 tbsp maple syrup
1 tbsp Dijon mustard
2 sweet potatoes
1 tbsp parsley (Chopped)
1 tbsp olive oil
½ cup goat cheese (Crumbled)
2 garlic cloves (minced)
1 tsp thyme
¼ tsp red pepper flakes
½ cup chicken broth
1 shallot (Minced)
1 ¼ cups pumpkin puree

Method
Spiralize the sweet potatoes to make noodles, then add them to a food processor. Pulse so the noodles become rice-like. Set to one side. Preheat your oven to 425 Fahrenheit. Season the pork chops, and add them to a baking sheet that's been lined with parchment. Now take a bowl, and add the pecans, mustard, maple syrup and chili powder, stir well, and brush this mixture over the pork chops (On both sides).

Add the pork chops to the oven and cook for about 15 minutes, or until they are thoroughly cooked. Remove the chops from the skillet, and pour the juice into a container and set to one side.

Now add the oil to the skillet and heat on a medium heat. Then add the shallots, garlic, and red pepper flakes, and cook for 1 minute. Add the rice, and season. Cook for 2 minutes, stirring as you do. Now add the thyme, broth and pumpkin, and cook for 5 minutes, or until the rice is soft. Remove the skillet from the heat, and the cheese, and mix well. Now divide the risotto between 4 plates or bowls, and add a pork chop on top. Take the juices and pour them over the pork chops, and sprinkle the parsley on top. Serve.

Mustard & Honey Salmon With Turnip Risotto

Serves: 2-3

Ingredients:
3, 3 ounce salmon fillets
1 ½ tbsp parsley (Chopped)
1 tbsp Dijon mustard
¼ cup Parmesan (Grated)
1 tsp honey
½ cup vegetable broth
2 turnips
2 sprigs thyme
1 tbsp olive oil
1 tbsp shallots (Minced)
5 ounces Portobello mushrooms (Sliced)
1 garlic clove (Minced)
Salt & pepper

Method
Spiralize the turnips to make noodles, then add them to a food processor. Pulse so the noodles become rice-like. Set to one side. Preheat your oven to 425 Fahrenheit, and place some parchment on a baking sheet. When the oven has heated, add the filets to the baking sheet. Now place the honey and mustard in a bowl, and mix well. Brush the honey mix on the filet's, and add them to the oven for 15 minutes, or until they are cooked to your satisfaction.

Now add the olive oil to a skillet, and heat it on a medium- low heat. Add the shallots, mushrooms, and garlic. Stir well. Season, and cook for about 3-4 minutes, or until the mushrooms are wilting a little. Add the rice, stir, and add the thyme, stir again, and season. Cook for about 5 minutes, or until the rice is soft.

Now add the broth, stir, and allow it to reduce. This should take about 5 minutes. Add the Parmesan and ½ the parsley, and cook until the cheese is melted. Serve with the remainder of the parsley sprinkled over the top.

Butternut Squash Risotto With Egg & Bacon

Serves: 4

Ingredients:
4 bacon strips
¼ cup Havarti cheese (Shredded)
4 eggs
¼ cup mild cheddar
2 tbsp parsley (Minced)
½ cup chicken broth
1 butternut squash
Salt & pepper
1 tbsp olive oil
2 garlic cloves (Minced)

Method
Spiralize the butternut squash to make noodles, then add them to a food processor. Pulse so the noodles become rice-like. Set to one side. Take a skillet, and heat it on a medium-high heat. Add the bacon and cook for about 10 minutes, or until it's crispy, and set to one side. Heat the oil in a pot on a medium heat, and then add the garlic. Cook the garlic for 30 seconds, and add the rice, season, and stir. Cook for about 2 minutes, and stir in the broth. Simmer on a low heat, and cook for 10 minutes, or until the broth is reduced.

Take the pot off the heat and add the cheeses. Stir well, and add the bacon, and stir again. Now take the skillet that you cooked the bacon in, and wipe it clean, place it on a medium-high heat, and add the eggs. Cook as per your satisfaction, and then set the eggs to one side. Add the risotto to some plates, place the eggs on top, and sprinkle the parsley on top of the eggs. Serve.

Chicken Sausages With Sweet Potato Rice
Serves: 2

Ingredients:
½ tbsp olive oil
Salt & pepper
5 ounces chicken sausages (Chopped)
½ tsp smoked paprika
½ yellow bell pepper (Chopped)
½ tsp oregano
½ red bell pepper (Chopped)
1 tbsp tomato paste
1 sweet potato
½ tbsp chicken broth
¼ cup chicken broth
1 garlic clove (Minced)
¼ cup red onion (Chopped)
1 celery stalk (Diced)

Method
Spiralize the sweet potato to make noodles, then add them to a food processor. Pulse so the noodles become rice-like. Set to one side. Add the sausages and peppers to an oiled skillet on a medium heat. Cook for about 5 minutes, or until the sausages are browned. Add the sausages and peppers to a plate, and allow them to cool. Add the garlic, onions and celery to the skillet, and cook for 30 seconds. Now add ½ tbsp chicken broth, and allow to cook for 2 minutes, or until the onions are translucent.

Add the tomato paste, stir, and add the rice, paprika, oregano, and salt & pepper. Stir well, and cook for 1 minute. Add the rest of the chicken broth, and stir again. Cover and cook for 5 minutes, stirring frequently. Add the peppers and sausages to the skillet, cook for a few more minutes, or until the rice is done. Add the parsley, stir, and serve.

Carrot Risotto With Bacon
Serves: 1

Ingredients:
2 slices bacon
1 tsp parsley
2 carrots
Pepper
1 tsp garlic (Minced)
1 tbsp lemon juice
½ cup leeks (Sliced)
½ cup vegetable broth
1 tbsp vegetable broth

Method
Spiralize the carrots to make noodles, then add them to a food processor. Pulse so the noodles become rice-like. Set to one side. Place a skillet on a medium heat, and spray with some cooking spray. Now add the bacon and cook for 5 minutes, or until it's about to turn crispy. Remove the bacon and set to one side. Now add the leeks and garlic to the skillet and cook for 1 minute, add 1 tbsp vegetable broth, and stir well. Now add the rice and lemon juice, stir again, season, stir once more, and cook for 1 minute.

Add the remaining vegetable broth, reduce it until all of the liquid has been absorbed. Now dice the bacon, and fold it into the rice. Stir well, sprinkle the parsley on top, and serve.

Carrot Rice With Jalapeño & Charred Peppers

Serves: 2

Ingredients:
2 plum tomatoes (De-seeded, chopped)
1 avocado (Insides cubed)
Juice of 1 lime
2 tbsp cilantro (Chopped)
½ cup red onion (Diced)
1 red bell pepper
2 tbsp salted pepitas
1 carrot
¼ cup vegetable broth
1 garlic clove (Minced)
Salt & pepper
1 Jalapeño (De-seeded, minced)

Method
Spiralize the carrots to make noodles, then add them to a food processor. Pulse so the noodles become rice-like. Set to one side. Add the plum tomatoes, red onion, lime juice, avocado, and cilantro to a bowl, mix well, and set to one side. Now take the pepper, and add it to the stovetop. Heat on a high heat, and char it, making sure you rotate it now and again. The skin of the pepper needs to be black, once it is add it to a plastic container, place the lid on top, and allow it to steam in there for 5 minutes. Once 5 minutes is up, peel the pepper, and slice it into strips. Set to one side.

Heat the oil in a skillet, and add the garlic, cook for 30 seconds, and add the rice and Jalapeño, stir and season. Cook for a few minutes, and add the broth, and cook for 5 more minutes, or until the rice is soft. Divide the rice between a few bowls, top with the peppers and salsa, spoon on the pepitas, and serve.

Spicy Butternut Squash Rice With Shrimp
Serves: 4

Ingredients:
10 shrimp (De-veined, peeled)
2 tbsp parsley (Chopped)
2 red bell peppers (Diced)
½ cup chicken broth
2 tbsp olive oil
1 butternut squash
2 garlic cloves (Minced)
½ tsp chili powder
¼ tsp red pepper flakes
½ tsp smoked paprika
1 cup white onion (Diced)
Salt & pepper
14 ounces tomatoes (Diced)

Method
Spiralize the butternut squash to make noodles, then add them to a food processor. Pulse so the noodles become rice-like. Set to one side. Add the olive oil to a skillet, and turn the heat up to medium, add the red pepper flakes, onion, and garlic, stir and cook for 1 minute, and add the red peppers. Cook for a few more minutes, and add the rice, salt & pepper, smoked paprika, chili powder, and tomatoes. Stir well, and cook until add of the tomato juices have been absorbed.
Add the chicken broth, stir well, then add the shrimp. Stir again, and cook for 2 minutes, turn the shrimps

over, cook for 2 more minutes, and stir. Add the parsley, stir again, and serve.

Butternut Squash Rice Stuffed Peppers With Chorizo

Serves: 4

Ingredients:
3 bell peppers (De-seeded, sliced lengthwise)
1 cup pepper jack cheese (Shredded)
2 chorizo sausages (Casings removed, crumbled)
½ butternut squash
1 avocado (Cubed)
1 cup chicken broth
1 tbsp olive oil
1 tsp smoked paprika
1 garlic clove (Minced)
½ tsp cumin
¼ tsp red pepper flakes
Salt
1/3 cup yellow onion (Diced)

Method
Spiralize the butternut squash to make noodles, then add them to a food processor. Pulse so the noodles become rice-like. Set to one side. Set your oven to broil, and place the peppers on a baking tray that's been sprayed with cooking spray. Broil the peppers for about 4 minutes, then take them out of the oven (Leave the broiler on). Now spray a skillet with cooking spray, and add the avocado and chorizo, and cook for 3 minutes, tossing frequently. Set to one side, and then add the onion, cook for 2 minutes, or until the onion is soft.

Now add the rice, cumin, salt and paprika to the skillet and stir well. Cook for 1 minute, and pour in half the broth, stir, allow to reduce, and then add ¼ cup broth, allow to reduce, then add the rest of the broth. Add the avocado and chorizo to the broth, stir, and then stuff the peppers with the rice mix. Pat down the rice with a spoon, and sprinkle the cheese on top. Now place the peppers back under the broiler, and broil for 3 minutes, or until the pepper is just about to burn. Remove from the broiler, and serve.

Pasta & Noodles

Zucchini Pasta With Sun Dried Tomatoes
Serves: 2

Ingredients:
4 chestnut mushrooms (Quartered)
Salt & pepper
2 tbsp coconut oil
1 cup sun dried tomatoes
½ cup olives (Sliced)
1 Jalapeño
3 zucchinis
½ cup vegetable broth
1 tsp apple cider vinegar
1 tsp garlic powder
1 tbsp olive oil

Method
Spiralize the zucchinis to make noodles, and set to one side. Preheat your oven to 400 Fahrenheit. Add the mushrooms, salt & pepper, and oil to a bowl and toss well to combine. Roast the mushrooms for 10 minutes. Add the sun dried tomatoes, pepper, broth, garlic powder, apple cider vinegar, olive oil, and olives to a blender, and blend until smooth. Now add the sauce to a pot, and heat on a medium heat. Add the zucchini, and cook for about 3 minutes, or until they are heated through. Spoon the zucchini and sauce

onto a plate, top with the olives and mushrooms.
Serve.

Beet Noodles With Pomegranate And Goat Cheese

Serves: 2

Ingredients:
2 beets
¼ cup pomegranate seeds
Salt & pepper
¼ cup goat cheese (Crumbled)
1 tbsp raw pepitas
1 tsp Dijon mustard
1 tsp honey
2 tbsp olive oil
1 tbsp apple cider vinegar

Method
Spiralize the beets to to make ribbons, and set to one side. Take a bowl, and add the mustard, some seasoning, the olive oil, apple cider vinegar, and honey, and stir well. Add the ribbons to a bowl, and pour the dressing over them. Now add the pepitas and ½ of the cheese, and toss well. Add the ribbons to a plate, sprinkle the rest of the cheese on top, and garnish with the pomegranate seeds.

Tuna & Cucumber Noodle Salad
Serves: 3

Ingredients:
1 cucumber
Salt & pepper
2 ½ cups tomato (Seeded, diced)
3 tbsp lemon juice
7 ounces tuna
¼ cup olive oil
1 ¼ cup red onion (Diced)
1 tsp cumin

Method
Spiralize the cucumber to make noodles, and set to one side. Now add the tomato, cumin, lemon juice, tuna and oil to a bowl and mix well. Add the noodles and mix well again. Season, toss well, and serve.

Sweet Potato & Coconut Curry
Serves: 2

Ingredients:
1 tbsp coconut oil
Salt
1 carrot (Peeled, sliced)
13 ½ ounces coconut milk
1 red bell pepper (Sliced)
½ tbsp yellow curry powder
1 cup broccoli (Chopped)
1 tsp ginger (Minced)
1/3 cup onion (Chopped)
1 sweet potato
1 mango (Diced)
¼ cup cilantro
2 tbsp red onion (Diced)
1 Thai red chili (Minced)
½ tsp apple cider vinegar.

Method
Spiralize the sweet potato to make noodles, and set to one side. Heat ½ tbsp coconut oil in a skillet on a medium heat and add the carrots. Stir well, and cook for 2-3 minutes, or until they are soft. Add the ginger, broccoli, onion, and pepper, and cook for 5 minutes, or until they start to go soft.

Now add the curry powder, and cook for 1 minute. Add the coconut milk, stir well, and season with a bit of salt, stir again.

Bring the temperature up to medium-high, and allow to boil, then reduce the heat to medium-low, and simmer for about 15 minutes until the sauce has thickened.

Now take the rest of the coconut oil, and heat it in a pot on a medium heat. Add the noodles, and cook for 10 minutes, or until they begin to wilt. Season, and set to one side. Add the Thai chili, cilantro, apple cider vinegar, and mango to a bowl, toss and season. Spoon the noodles onto a plate, pour on the sauce, and top with the mango, and any leftover cilantro. Serve.

Sweet Potato Enchilada
Serves: 3

Ingredients:
½ tbsp olive oil
1 cup Mozzarella
½ small onion (Chopped)
1 cup enchilada sauce
2 sweet potatoes
2 corn tortillas, (Cut into strips)
9 ounces black beans
6 ounces corn kernels
2 tbsp Greek yogurt
2 tbsp cilantro

Method
Spiralize the sweet potatoes to make noodles, and set to one side. Preheat your oven to 350 Fahrenheit. Now take a skillet, and heat the olive oil on a medium heat. Add the onion to the skillet, and cook until translucent (This should take about 5 minutes). Add the noodles, and cook for 10 minutes, or until they are cooked to your satisfaction. Add the garlic, and cook for 1 more minute.

Now stir in the corn, tortillas, beans and corn, along with the enchilada sauce, and ½ the cheese. Stir well. Sprinkle the rest of the cheese on top of the enchilada, and place it in the oven. Cook for 5 minutes, or until the cheese has melted. Remove from the oven, and top

with the Greek yogurt, and sprinkle on the cilantro.
Serve.

Chicken Zoodles With Parmesan & Tomato

Serves: 3

Ingredients:
½ tbsp butter
1 zucchini
350 g chicken thighs (Cut into strips)
Red chili flakes
2 ounces semi-dried tomato strips (In oil)
Cilantro
1 ½ ounces sun dried tomatoes (Chopped)
Salt
2 cloves garlic (Peeled, crushed)
½ cup Parmesan (Shaved)
½ cup thick cream

Method
Spiralize the zucchini to make spaghetti noodles, and set to one side. Now heat the butter in a skillet on a medium heat, and then add the chicken strips. Season with the salt, and fry the chicken until it's thoroughly cooked, and brown on all sides. This should take 5-8 minutes. Add all of the tomatoes, and then stir in 1 tbsp of the oil from the tomato jar. Add the garlic, and cook for 30 seconds.

Now reduce the heat to low, and add the cheese and cream. Simmer, and stir while the cheese melts. Sprinkle the salt, and some red chili flakes and cilantro. Stir well. Add the zoodles, and simmer until they are soft (About 5 minutes). Serve.

Thai Noodle Salad With Peanut & Lime Dressing

Serves: 4-6

Ingredients:
1 cucumber
½ cup peanuts (Chopped)
1 zucchini (Shredded)
½ cup cilantro (Chopped)
1 red bell pepper (De-seeded, chopped)
2 green onions (Chopped)
¼ cup creamy peanut butter
Juice of 1 lime
¼ cup canola oil
¼ tsp red pepper flakes
2 tbsp rice wine vinegar
1 tsp ginger (Grated)
2 tbsp honey
1 ½ tbsp soy sauce

Method
Spiralize the carrot and cucumber to make noodles, and set to one side. Add the zucchini, onions, cilantro, noodles, and bell pepper to a bowl, and mix well. Set to one side. Now add the soy sauce, peanut butter, red pepper flakes, vinegar, lime juice, honey and canola oil to a bowl and whisk well. Pour the sauce over the noodles, sprinkle the peanuts on top, and serve.

Singapore Zoodle Stir Fry With Chicken
Serves: 4

Ingredients:
½ cup light soy sauce
1 tsp white sugar
2 tbsp Chinese rice wine
½ tsp ginger (Grated)
2 cloves garlic (Minced)
9 ounces shrimp
3 zucchini
9 ounces chicken thigh filet's (Sliced, boneless, skinless)
3 ½ ounces snow peas
2 tbsp olive oil
2 ounces bean sprouts
2 eggs (Whisked, salt added)
1 red bell pepper (De-seeded, halved, sliced)
2 tsp curry powder
1 onion (Sliced)
2 green shallots (Trimmed, sliced)
Sprinkle of sesame seeds

Method
Spiralize the zucchinis to make noodles, and set to one side. In a bowl, add the soy sauce, rice wine, garlic, sugar and ginger. Whisk, and set to one side. Now take the shrimp and pat it dry, then add 2 tbsp of the sauce to the shrimp, and set to one. Take the chicken, add 1 tbsp of the sauce to it, stir well, and set to one side.

Heat 1 tsp oil in a skillet on a high heat, and add the eggs, and make an omelet. Once the omelet has been made, cut it up, into pieces, and using a spoon, take it out of the skillet. Set to one side.

Wipe the skillet clean, and then add the chicken. Cook for 3 minutes or until the chicken is thoroughly cooked. Add to a warm plate, and then fry the shrimp in the skillet for a few minutes, or until the shrimp has turned pink. Take the shrimp out of the skillet, and set to one side.

Now take the skillet, and heat the oil that's currently in there. Add 1 tsp curry powder, and fry it for about 30 seconds. Now add the vegetables, and fry for 3 minutes or until the snow peas and onion are soft. Add the zoodles and the rest of the sauce. Fry for 2 minutes, or until the zoodles are soft. Add the egg, shrimp and chicken, and mix well. Season, and sprinkle the sesame seeds and green onion on top. Serve.

Teriyaki Zoodles With Meatballs
Serves: 2

Ingredients:
¾ pound ground turkey
¼ cup soy sauce
2 tbsp soy sauce
¼ tsp salt
1 tbsp sesame seeds
1 tsp garlic powder
½ cup oats
1 ¼ tsp ginger
1 tsp corn starch
¼ tsp hot chili oil
1/8 tsp hot chili oil
2 tsp rice wine vinegar
2 tsp honey
2 ½ cups broccoli (Chopped)
4 zucchini
½ red pepper (Sliced)
3 garlic cloves (Minced)
Salt & pepper
¼ cup peanuts (Chopped)
2 tbsp cilantro

Method
Spiralize the zucchini to make thin noodles, and set to one side. Preheat your oven to 375 Fahrenheit, and line a baking sheet with some parchment. In a bowl add the salt, 2 tbsp soy sauce, ginger, garlic, corn starch, ¼ tsp chili oil, turkey and oats. Stir a little,

and shape into meatballs. Place the meatballs on the baking sheet, and sprinkle with the sesame seeds. Add to the oven, and bake for 15 minutes, set to one side.

Add the rest of the soy sauce, to a bowl and stir in the vinegar, remaining chili oil and honey. Whisk well, and set to one side. Now heat a pan on a medium-high heat, and spray it with cooking spray. Add the red peppers and broccoli, and cook until soft, this should take about 4 minutes. Add the garlic, stir, and season. Now add the zoodles and sauce, and cook for 2 more minutes. Serve with the meatballs on top, and garnish with the cilantro and peanuts.

Sweet Potato Noodle & Chick Pea Soup
Serves: 4

Ingredients:
1 tbsp coconut oil
Salt & pepper
2 tsp turmeric
½ cup parsley
2 tsp ginger
½ cup cilantro
1 tsp caraway seeds
5 cups water
1 tsp hot smoked paprika
3 lemon slices
½ tsp cinnamon
1 sweet potato
½ tsp nutmeg
1 cup lentils (Soaked)
1 pinch saffron (Soaked)
3 cups chickpeas
3 onions (Diced)
6 ounces tomato paste
1 tsp sea salt
14 ounces whole tomatoes

Method
Spiralize the sweet potato to make noodles with the
thickness of your choice, and set to one side. Add the
coconut oil to a pot on a medium-high heat, and add
the nutmeg, cinnamon, turmeric, paprika, ginger, and
caraway. Stir and cook for 1 minute, or until fragrant.

Turn the heat down to medium, and add the salt and onions. Stir, and cook for 10 minutes. Add the saffron, tomatoes, lentils, lemon slices, chickpeas, tomato paste and water, and bring it to a boil. Reduce the heat to a simmer, and cook for 20-25 minutes or until the lentils are soft.

Add the herbs and noodles to the pot, and stir well. Simmer for 5 minutes, and season. Serve.

Apple & Kohlrabi Noodle Salad With Cranberries

Serves: 1

Ingredients:
1 Kohlrabi
Salt & pepper
1 apple
1 tbsp Dijon mustard
¼ cup goat cheese (Crumbled)
3 tbsp olive oil
2 tbsp walnuts (Chopped)
1 tbsp red wine vinegar
1 tbsp dried cranberries
2 tbsp honey
1 handful arugula

Method
Spiralize the kohlrabi and apple to make noodles, and set to one side. Now add the honey, salt & pepper, olive oil and mustard to a bowl, and whisk well. Add the noodles to a bowl, and pour the dressing over the top. Sprinkle on the cheese, walnuts and cranberries, and serve.

Arugula And Pear Noodle Salad
Serves: 2

Ingredients:
¼ cup Greek yogurt
Salt & pepper
3 tbsp balsamic vinegar
1 tbsp honey
1 tsp Dijon mustard
2 Bosc pears
½ cup Wisconsin blue cheese
4 cups baby arugula
¾ cup walnuts

Method
Spiralize the pears to make thick noodles, and set to
one side. Add the yogurt, vinegar, mustard, honey,
and seasoning to a bowl and whisk well. Now take
another bowl, and add the cheese and walnuts along
with the noodles, and toss to combine. Mix the
dressing with the noodles, and serve.

Carrot & Cucumber Noodle Thai Salad

Serves: 2

Ingredients:
3 tbsp olive oil
1 tsp red pepper flakes
1 tbsp peanut butter
1 tsp peanut butter
Salt & pepper
1 tsp soy sauce
Just and zest of a lime
1 tsp sesame seed oil
1 tsp honey
1 cucumber
½ cup sunflower seeds
2 carrots
¾ cup edamame beans
Handful cilantro (Chopped)
1 avocado (Cubed)
Handful mint (Chopped)

Method
Spiralize the cucumber and carrots to make noodles, and set to one side. Add the olive oil, peanut butter, soy sauce, sesame oil, honey, lime zest & juice, salt & pepper, and red pepper flakes to a bowl. Mix well. Add the rest of the ingredients, and toss well. Serve.

Greek-Style Cucumber Noodle Salad
Serves: 2

Ingredients:
2 cucumbers
Salt & pepper
1 cup grape tomatoes (Halved)
½ cup Feta cheese (Crumbled)
½ cup pitted olives (Chopped)
4 tbsp hummus
¼ red onion (Sliced)

Method
Spiralize the cucumbers to make noodles, and add them to a bowl. Add the onion, tomatoes and olives, and add the hummus to the middle of the noodles. Sprinkle the cheese over the top, and season. Serve.

Chicken Chow Mein Noodles
Serves: 4

Ingredients:
3 zucchini
¼ cup cilantro (Chopped)
1 chicken breast (Chopped)
2 cups snow peas, carrot slices, bok choy
2 cloves garlic (Minced)
1 red bell pepper
½ tsp ginger
1 yellow bell pepper
½ cup water
½ tsp sesame oil
½ tbsp corn starch
1 ½ tsp miso paste
1 ½ tbsp soy sauce
1 ½ tsp honey
1 tbsp oyster flavored sauce
2 tsp rice wine

Method
Season the chicken and then heat 1 tsp olive oil in a skillet on a medium-high heat. Add the chicken and cook for 3-4 minutes, or until it's browned. Add to a plate, and set to one side. Whisk the water, corn starch, soy sauce, oyster sauce, rice wine, honey, misto paste and sesame oil together. Set to one side.

Add 1 tsp olive oil to the skillet, and sauté the peppers, ginger, snow peas, garlic, and bok choy. Stir and cook for 2 minutes. Add the noodles and chicken, and pour the sauce over the noodles. Cook until the sauce becomes thick, this should take a few minutes. Serve with the cilantro sprinkled on top. Spiralize the zucchini to make noodles, and set to one side.

Shrimp Scampi
Serves: 4

Ingredients:
1 pound shrimp (Raw)
2 tbsp butter
8 cloves garlic (Diced)
Pepper
4 zucchini
¼ cup Parmesan

Method:
Spiralize zucchini to create noodles, and set to one side. Add the butter to a pan, and melt, then add the garlic and cook on a medium heat for 30 seconds. Add the shrimp and zucchini noodles, and stir until the shrimp is pink. Sprinkle some Parmesan on top, season and serve.

Buffalo Chicken Zoodle Bake

Serves: 5

Ingredients:
1 pound chicken breast (Boneless, skinless, chopped)
2 zucchinis
¼ tsp garlic powder
½ cup sour cream
3 tbsp pumpkin puree
1 ½ tbsp Parmesan
2 tbsp red bell pepper (Chopped)
1/3 cup cheddar
1 ½ tbsp red pepper sauce
1 tbsp butter
½ tsp ground mustard

Method
Spiralize the zucchini to create thin noodles, and set to one side. Preheat your oven to 400 Fahrenheit, and grease a casserole dish. Heat the butter in a pan with the sour cream, pumpkin puree, Parmesan, garlic powder, red pepper sauce and mustard. Stir well, and remove from the heat. Now add the noodles to the casserole dish, and place the celery and chicken on top. Sprinkle the pepper over the chicken, and cook for 30 minutes. Once 30 minutes is up, remove the dish from the oven, and sprinkle the cheddar on top. Allow to cool for a few minutes, and then serve.

Avocado & Spinach Pasta
Serves: 4

Ingredients:
1 avocado
1 zucchini
¾ cup water
1/3 cup basil
¼ cup Parmesan (Shredded)
1 clove garlic
½ cup pecans
1 cup spinach
Salt & pepper
1 tbsp lemon juice

Method
Spiralize the avocado and zucchini to create noodles, and set to one side.

Add all of the ingredients apart from the noodles to a blender, and blend until smooth. Now add the noodles to a pan that's been sprayed with cooking spray, and cook them for 10 minutes on a medium heat, or until they're soft. Once the noodles are cooked, add them to a plate, and spoon the sauce over the top. Sprinkle with some cilantro, and serve.

Zucchini Pasta

Serves: 4

Ingredients:
6 zucchini
Salt & pepper

Method
Spiralize the zucchini to create thin noodles or ribbons, and then add them to a stock pot. Add enough water to cover the zucchini, and bring it to a boil. Remove from the heat, and strain the water off. Sprinkle with the salt & pepper, and serve.

Carrot Noodles & Chicken With Peanut Sauce
Serves: 1

Ingredients:
5 carrots
½ tbsp soy sauce
1 ½ cloves garlic
1 tbsp sesame oil
½ tbsp ginger
½ tbsp apple cider vinegar
3 green onions (Chopped)
2 tbsp peanut butter
1 ½ tbsp maple syrup
½ chicken (Chopped)

Method
Spiralize the carrot to create thin noodles, and set to one side. Now take a bowl, and add half the sesame oil, all the peanut butter, ginger, soy sauce and vinegar, and stir well. Set to one side.

Now heat a skillet on a medium heat, and add the rest of the sesame oil. Add the green onions, garlic and chicken, and stir. Add the noodles and cook until they are tender (This should take about 10 minutes). Once the noodles are done, remove from the skillet and set to one side. Cook the chicken for a further 10-15 minutes, or until it's cooked thoroughly.

Once the chicken is done, add it to a bowl. Place the noodles back into the skillet, add the peanut sauce and stir until it's heated through (About 5 minutes). Now pour the noodles and sauce over the chicken. Serve.

Conclusion

As you can see, there are some very tasty spiralizer recipes around. It is entirely possible for you to use your Spiralizer every single day, and for every single meal.

It's not that hard to make delicious and nutritious meals if you have the right equipment. This is why it makes perfect sense to get your hands on a Spiralizer so you too can create some tasty dishes.

Please feel free to experiment with recipe ideas, and don't be afraid to swap ingredients around should you wish to. Just make sure you put your Spiralizer to good use, so you and your family can enjoy exciting and healthy meals any time you wish.

Thank You

Before you go, we would like to say a warm "THANK YOU" on behalf of the Vigor & Belle family! We started this brand to help our customers live healthier, more vibrant lives and we hope that this book has served you in many ways.

If you enjoyed this book, then we'd like to ask you for a favor!

Please take a moment and leave a review for this book after you turn the page.

This feedback is crucial for us to continue to help you to live a healthier, happier and more vibrant lifestyle! If you loved this book, we would love to hear from you!

Live Healthy & Stay Beautiful,

The vigor&belle Family

17995379R00092

Printed in Poland
by Amazon Fulfillment
Poland Sp. z o.o., Wrocław